Praise for
Girl at the End of the World

"What a story! *Girl at the End of the World* is witty, insightful, courageous, and compelling, the sort of book you plan to read in a week but finish in a day. Elizabeth Esther is a master storyteller who describes her journey out of fundamentalism with a powerful mix of tenderness and guts. With this debut, Esther sets herself apart as a remarkable writer and remarkable woman. This book is a gift, and I cannot commend it enough."

——RACHEL HELD EVANS, blogger and author of *A Year of Biblical Womanhood*

"Sometimes hilarious, sometimes tragic, *Girl at the End of the World* provides an unflinching look at life growing up inside a fundamentalist cult. Elizabeth Esther's honest and vulnerable account of her childhood, and the effects of her parents' religious zeal, is both fascinating and poignant. I couldn't put this book down. It will provide hope to anyone recovering from an upbringing where religiosity was emphasized over a relationship with God."

——KRISTEN HOWERTON, author of RageAgainsttheMinivan.com

"*Girl at the End of the World* is an unforgettable mem[...] [...]e-knuckled its pages as I traveled through Elizabeth Esth[...] [...] childhood. I cheered for her when she finally f[...] [...] It's eye-opening, powerfully written, and [...] [...] conversation about fundamentalism[...]

——JASON BOYETT, author o[...]

"Elizabeth Esther's story is a powerful a[...] [...]nt, and she's told it beautifully. As I read, I thought of my own memories of growing up in an evangelical church and wondered how they've made me the person I am today. This book is a reminder that God is good and that He can redeem any story for His beloved children—or as Elizabeth says, that 'God is big enough to meet us anywhere.' I'm so glad she has bravely told her tale."

—Tsh Oxenreider, author of *Notes from a Blue Bike:*
The Art of Living Intentionally in a Chaotic World

"There is life on every page. *Girl at the End of the World* is evidence that sometimes our scars make the most beautiful art."

—Josh James Riebock, author of *Heroes and Monsters*

"A delightful book: funny and wise and rich with insight about God and faith. Even while Elizabeth tells the darker threads of her story, her innocence, wit, and spiritual exuberance shine brightly."

—Matthew Paul Turner, author of *Churched*
and *Our Great Big American God*

"A memoir about childhood should not read like a seat-of-the-pants thriller, but Elizabeth Esther's does. And that's scary. I found myself wishing I could reach through the pages and hug that cowering, desperate girl, and tell her that God truly loves her. I'm so glad she knows His devotion now, and so grateful that she is sharing her story so that we, as God's ambassadors, can make sure abuse in the name of 'child training' never happens again."

—Sheila Wray Gregoire, author and blogger
at ToLoveHonorandVacuum.com

"Elizabeth shares with candor, wit, and near flawless writing about the religion she was so deeply hurt by. Her story is heartbreaking, yet redemptive, and we would all do well to pay attention to how religion without the love, grace, and truth of Jesus Christ is an empty and destructive force."

—Sarah Mae, author of *Desperate: Hope for the*
Mom Who Needs to Breathe

GIRL
AT THE
END
OF THE
WORLD

GIRL
AT THE
END
OF THE
WORLD

My Escape
from Fundamentalism
in Search of Faith with a Future

ELIZABETH ESTHER

CONVERGENT
BOOKS

GIRL AT THE END OF THE WORLD
PUBLISHED BY CONVERGENT BOOKS

Trade Paperback ISBN 978-0-307-73187-6
eBook ISBN 978-0-307-73188-3

Copyright © 2014 by Elizabeth Esther

Cover design by Kelly L. Howard; cover photography by Charles Gullung

Published in the United States by Convergent Books, an imprint of the Crown Publishing Group, a division of Random House LLC, New York, a Penguin Random House Company.

CONVERGENT BOOKS and its open book colophon are trademarks of Random House LLC.

Library of Congress Cataloging-in-Publication Data
Esther, Elizabeth.
    Girl at the end of the world : my escape from fundamentalism and search for faith with a future / Elizabeth Esther.—First Edition.
        pages cm
    ISBN 978-0-307-73187-6—ISBN 978-0-307-73188-3 (electronic) 1. Esther, Elizabeth. 2. Christian biography. 3. Religious fundamentalism—Biography. 4. Cults. 5. Psychological abuse—Religious aspects—Christianity. I. Title.
    BR1725.E84A3 2014
    277.3'083092—dc23
    [B]

                                                                    2013043785

Printed in the United States of America
2014—First Edition

10 9 8 7 6 5 4 3 2 1

SPECIAL SALES
Most Convergent books are available at special quantity discounts when purchased in bulk by corporations, organizations, and special-interest groups. Custom imprinting or excerpting can also be done to fit special needs. For information, please e-mail SpecialMarkets@Convergent Books.com or call 1-800-603-7051.

For Sean Paddock, Lydia Schatz, and Hana Alemu Williams.
Requiescat in pace, precious little ones.

Contents

PART
THREE

PART
ONE

Brainwashed

I am ready to die for Jesus. I am nine years old.

I clutch my little white Bible to my chest and step up on a plastic milk crate. Once again I'm ready to prove that I'm not ashamed of the gospel. If I can preach on this street corner and withstand the heckling of sinners, I'll show everyone I'm ready to be a martyr for the Lord.

I swallow hard and try to smile. I tell myself that God speaks through the mouths of babies. And I'm not a baby. I'm *nine.*

"Praise the Lord!" I shout. Nobody looks at me. "Praise *the Lord*!" I shout again.

Nothing.

This flummoxes me. I've preached all over the United States with my parents—to tourists at the 1984 Olympics in Los Angeles, gay-rights activists in San Francisco, and college students in Midwest university towns—but this Rhode Island crowd is the toughest. Maybe Dad is right: maybe the most hardhearted sinners are East Coast Catholic liberals.

There is a bookstore nearby, and I redirect my sermon to the Brown University students walking toward it. "I want to share with you the glorious message of our Lord Jesus Christ!"

Street-preaching tip: shout the name of Jesus, and people will look at you.

Suddenly, eyes are on me. I try to smile again—"Always look pleasant!" Mom says—but the East Coast humidity sits heavy on my shoulders like a hot, wet blanket. I feel smothered.

I glance at Dad, and he gives me a boisterous thumbs-up. He says there's no greater honor than being persecuted for my faith. I *want* somebody to heckle me. Nothing would make my dad happier.

I open my Bible to the bookmarked spot and hold it open in front of me. I pretend to read the words aloud even though I know them from memory. In my family, preaching is a competitive sport. Before I was reading, I could rattle off the books of the Bible. By age five I could preach a three-point gospel message in one minute. Damnation to salvation in sixty seconds flat.

"In Romans 3:23, the Bible says, 'For all have sinned and fallen short of the glory of God'!" I shout.

Street-preaching tip: always use the phrase *the Bible says* to make your words sound as if they come straight from God. And always give 'em the bad news first, because until sinners understand how wicked they are and how desperately they need Jesus, they won't repent.

"God sent his only begotten Son, Jesus, to die for our sins!" I glance at the gathering crowd and decide to ratchet it up a notch. "The Bible says it is appointed unto man once to die and then *the judgment*!"

A plain-faced woman with wiry gray hair is eating ice cream on a nearby street bench. I point my finger at her. "*You* might die today!"

She stops midlick and raises a curious eyebrow at me.

"But there's good news! The Bible says the free gift of God is eternal life through Jesus Christ our Lord!'"

The woman shakes her head and looks away. I direct my last line at a few people standing around. "Please ask Jesus into your heart today!"

I'm done. I step off the milk crate and dash to Mom, who is standing nearby holding a stack of Bible study invitations.

"Good job, Elizabeth," Mom says and hands me some invitations. "Now help me pass these out."

Whenever we land in a new city to preach the gospel, Dad rents a house near a local university and then draws people to our home Bible study by holding these open-air preaching sessions and community outreaches. Our goal is to plant a new church in six weeks. I turn to hand out the invitations, but someone is yelling.

"Look here, man!" a lady shouts. "What you're doing to your little girl is wrong!"

I turn to see the wiry-haired ice-cream lady standing in front of Dad, jabbing a finger in his face. "This is brainwashing!"

"Whoa, ma'am. Please calm down." Dad has his hands up in a gesture of surrender.

"Don't tell me to calm down! You're not in charge of me!"

"Hey, hey. There's no need to yell." Dad chuckles, unruffled. "I'm more than happy to have a conversation with you. Would you like some cookies? Maybe a lemonade?" Dad gestures at Mom to serve something from the snacks we've set up on a card table.

The angry lady waves her off. "I don't want any of your damned *Kool-Aid*! I want you to *listen* to me for one goddamned minute."

"Well, I'm afraid we can't have a reasonable conversation if you insist on yelling and using foul language," Dad replies, crossing his arms over his chest. He leans back on his heels and smiles benignly. I clutch Mom's skirt.

The woman glances at me and then lowers her voice a notch. She leans toward Dad. "Look," she growls, "it's fine for you to have your religion. But sticking your little girl up there on a stage and making her yell at people? That's wrong! You're teaching her to manipulate people through fear. You're brainwashing her!"

Dad raises his eyebrows, but his voice remains calm. "With all due respect, you don't know me or my daughter. There's no way you can prove what you're saying."

"I don't need to prove anything to you!" the woman snaps. "I know abuse and manipulation when I see it. I should report you to Child Protective Services!"

"Well, we've got nothin' to hide," Dad says, still smiling. "And anyway, I can think of a lot worse things than being brainwashed to love Jesus!"

The lady spins on her heels and stalks away, muttering obscenities.

"May God richly bless ya!" Dad calls after her.

She whips back around, glares at Dad, and then looks directly at me. For one quick second, her face softens. Dad steps forward.

"Don't be afraid to think for yourself!" she shouts before Dad blocks my view.

Mom claps her hands over my ears. But it's too late. I already heard it. *Don't be afraid to think for yourself.*

I don't even know what that means.

I was raised in a homegrown, fundamentalist Christian group—which is just a shorthand way of saying I'm classically trained in apocalypse stockpiling, street preaching, and the King James Version of the Bible. I know hundreds of obscure nineteenth-century hymns by heart and have such razor-sharp "modesty vision" that I can spot a miniskirt a mile away.

Verily, verily I say unto thee, none of these highly specialized skills ever got me a job, but at least I'm all set for the End of the World. *Selah.*

I was born in 1977, just a few years after my paternal grandfather, George Geftakys, began holding informal Bible studies in his living room. An insurance salesman and part-time preacher, he had never been officially ordained. He said the only requirement for serving God was "hearing the call of Jesus" and having the anointing of the Holy Spirit. True disciples of Christ didn't need seminary or the approval of "hypocritical, organized religion" in order to do the Lord's work. George Geftakys— known as Papa George to family—claimed his authority came straight from God. Which was just another way of saying he ordained himself.

Conveniently, self-ordination also meant Papa George was the final authority on everything and answered to no one. Papa George was pretty much a prophet, priest, and king all rolled into one.

Still, he found a way to harness the Jesus Movement energy and create his own personal brand of Christianity. Our basic beliefs were similar to Baptists' but with Papa George's added emphasis on personal holiness, evangelism, and End of the World prophecy. From our grass-roots start as a Bible study in Papa George's living room, The Assembly—as we came to be known—grew to include about fifty sister Assemblies throughout the United States, Canada, Mexico, Europe, and Africa.

In the beginning, The Assembly was vibrant, energetic, and revolutionary. It was *groovy*. The social experimentation of the sixties had broken down the walls of tired old religion, and a new generation was falling in love with Jesus. Roaring out of Southern California like wildfire, the Jesus Movement upended traditional Christian denominations and challenged the religious establishment.

Empty, impersonal ritual was replaced with charismatic, personal experiences. Written prayers gave way to spontaneous individual expression of praise. Preachers like my grandfather insisted traditional churches had become false mediators and God was allowing an outpouring of the Holy Spirit in order to bring people back into direct contact with Jesus.

Among those drawn by my grandfather's charisma and Bible preaching was my mother, a beautiful debutante and former high school cheerleader. She'd grown up in Baptist churches, but as a college freshman, she was looking for something different, something more real. She stumbled across a Bible study being held at California State University, Fullerton, and was immediately dazzled by Papa George's fiery preaching. She also met my dad at that Bible study. He was Papa George's younger son.

My parents were an unlikely pair. Dad was a college dropout; Mom was a straight-A student. He was gregarious and she was an introvert.

Mom told me the first time she saw my dad he was wearing tattered army fatigues, huarache sandals, and—here Mom crinkled her nose in disgust—"he'd *hitchhiked* to the Bible study."

But they fell in love over studying the Bible, all-night prayer meetings, and living "100 percent sold-out for Jesus."

As Mom liked to say with a nostalgic sigh, "In the early days, we didn't have anything but Jesus." Not having anything but Jesus was what everyone *always* talked about when they reminisced about The Assembly's early years. They fondly remembered being enthusiastic young college students in the early seventies, radically redefining Christianity in a new, exciting way. They saw themselves as faith revolutionaries on the cusp of a huge revival, which would usher in the return of Jesus to Earth. Everyone was finding Jesus and getting saved, baptizing each other in the Pacific Ocean, getting married, and starting families.

Sometimes, when we were traveling across the United States preaching the gospel, my parents would get all flushed with Jesus fervor, clasp hands, and burst into hymns in two-part harmony. These wild preaching sessions were inevitably followed by noisy lovemaking in whatever cheap hotel room we were renting—with me plugging my ears and pretending to be asleep in the other bed.

It was all very exciting for them, I suppose. But as a child growing up in The Assembly, I had a far different experience.

As with most revolutions, the idealistic dream that had initially ignited our little band of born-again Christians gradually hardened into a rigid lifestyle. Ironically, by the mideighties, we had morphed to become nearly indistinguishable from the legalistic, organized religion we'd rejected in the first place.

What I remember most are the increasingly strict rules and the insular, fundamentalist traditions we developed. Papa George's interpretation of the Bible was hyperliteral: he demanded complete and total loyalty— spiritualizing this conformity as "unity in Christ." Children were spanked from six months old until they were teenagers. Women were required to dress very modestly and behave within strict gender roles. Everything, from how we ordered our daily schedules to our tone of voice, was monitored. The only person who wasn't held accountable for anything was Papa George.

This is why, when people ask me why I call The Assembly a cult, I say it's because we operated like one. Cults aren't so much about beliefs as they are about methods and behavior. According to cult researchers, it is the emotional seizing of people's trust, thoughts, and choices that identifies a cult. The Assembly wins on all counts.

Fundamentalism that becomes cultish destroys the God-given freedom of each person. Usually this is accomplished through fear. In my own experience, the most detrimental aspect of my childhood was our preoccupation with End of the World theology. Even though my grandfather was never quite certain whether Christians would be persecuted before or after the Rapture, the End of the World was coming soon, and we had to stay prepared.

Indeed, everything in our lives was oriented toward the End of the World. Thus, my parents never owned a home, never had a savings account, and never invested toward retirement. They didn't save money to send me to college because planning for the future was irrelevant when there *was* no future. That's why by age nine I had simply resigned myself to dying for Jesus.

"What's brainwashing?" I ask.

Dad squats in front of me, his face a huge, beaming smile. "Oh, don't you worry about that crazy feminist, Wiz," he says, calling me by the nickname he's had for me since I was a toddler. "Keep your eye on the prize; you just endured persecution. What a privilege! I bet you just earned yourself a huge crown of glory!"

Mom whispers something in Dad's ear, and he shakes his head. "No, no. Don't worry about that," he says. "If the cops show up, I'll tell them I was exercising my constitutional right to freedom of speech and some crabby feminist didn't like it."

Mom leans against Dad, and he winks at me. "Mama, how 'bout you go get Wiz some frozen lemonade? She's earned it!"

I feel relief wash over me. I've preached the gospel and suffered for Jesus. Dad and God are proud of me. If Dad is right about this whole being-persecuted-for-Jesus thing, I've just scored some major heavenly swag.

The adults in our fundamentalist church are forever fantasizing about what they'll get in heaven: new bodies, mansions, and crowns of glory. Dad likes to say he wants beachfront property on the Crystal Sea.

As Mom walks me to the frozen-lemonade shop, I dream about the heavenly prizes I've just won. I don't dare say it aloud because Mom will scold me for desiring "things of this world," but if I'm being honest, all I really want is a television, a Happy Meal, and a Christmas Barbie.

Apocalypse Prep 101

Dad is putting together an apocalypse survival plan. He makes me promise to keep it a secret.

"If anyone asks what we're doing, just say we're doing earthquake prep," he says. "The State is always watching, Wiz. Nobody needs to know how we're gonna outwit the Antichrist."

The first phase of our plan includes scouting out a secret family meeting spot. Dad says it needs to be within walking distance of home, easily accessible by foot, but also hidden from plain view. Since we live in Fullerton, a sprawling university city about thirty miles south of Los Angeles, our options are limited to local parks.

One afternoon I am reading on the living room couch when Dad sneaks in the front door, cowboy hat pulled low over his forehead. He closes the door softly behind him, gesturing at me to keep quiet. Glancing around, he slides along the wall toward me.

"Go check the front windows," he whispers. "Make sure no servants of the State are outside."

Sometimes I'm not sure whether Dad is playing up the intrigue to make our adventures more fun or truly worried about government spies. Usually, it's both. So I check the front windows. "Coast is clear, Dad."

He nods. "Good. Then go get in the car, Wiz. I have something to show you. Use the back door. Act normal; be quick."

I saunter out of the house and then break into a run, dashing to the Dodge van. My fingers tremble as I fasten my seat belt. *Where is he taking me? Has he found our secret meeting spot?* I know he is worried about something because earlier that morning he'd emerged from his study looking red eyed and weary.

"Well, Wiz," he'd said with a sigh. "It doesn't really matter when or how the Rapture happens. Either way, we gotta stay prepared."

I'd nodded soberly, knowing he'd been researching the topic for months. Dad had amassed a veritable library of books and pamphlets on End Times prophecy. He pored over *The Late Great Planet Earth* and *88 Reasons Why the Rapture Will Be in 1988*. He studied competing theories and apocalyptic timetables, trying to discern whether the Great Tribulation would follow or precede the Rapture.

As fundamentalists, we liked to read with the Bible in one hand and a newspaper in the other. We were always looking for signs that The End was near. Would credit cards usher in a global currency? Would the growing popularity of tattoos normalize body markings and lead to the mark of the Beast? Was the Catholic Church the Whore of Babylon?

In the past year, Papa George had been preaching that Something Big was gonna happen in 1988 because it was Israel's fortieth anniversary. The number forty, after all, carried huge biblical significance. Papa George said the signs were clear. Jesus was returning to Earth in 1988.

I'd followed Dad into the kitchen and watched him fill a glass with tap water. He slugged it down and refilled it. Sometimes he got so lost in Scripture study that he forgot to eat or drink.

"There's no use trying to pinpoint exact days and times," Dad said, plunking his empty glass on the counter. "Even Jesus didn't know the day or hour!"

Now, as I wait for Dad in the Dodge van, I can't help wondering if he's finally found a suitable secret family-meeting spot. I feel a little thrill of excitement. Finally! It is becoming real. I am so sick of waiting and worrying for The End to happen. It feels good to finally do something about it.

Dad drives us around Fullerton for a while, constantly checking his rearview mirror to see if we are being followed. He avoids main roads and sticks to side streets, doubling back a couple of times to throw off any would-be followers. "You can never be too careful," he says.

While we drive he rattles off a list of strategies for eluding capture: never take a window seat in a restaurant, always sit where you can see the front door, stay alert at all times. After about twenty minutes of circuitous driving, we end up a couple of miles from home at Hillcrest Park.

Dad has deep, fond memories of Hillcrest Park. In the early days of The Assembly, Papa George held meetings in the park's recreation center, and several young couples were married there, including Mom and Dad. Each summer, we held tent meetings on the wide grassy lawn fronting Harbor Boulevard. As we pull into the parking lot near the rec center, he smiles at me conspiratorially.

Dad edges the van into a spot under a huge, overgrown pepper tree. We wait a few minutes. Nobody has followed us, and on this weekday afternoon, the park is deserted.

"Okay, let's go," Dad says. "But keep quiet and move quick."

We hop out of the van and scurry up a flight of old stone steps leading into an overgrown area of the park. Dad takes the steps two at a time and then waits for me at the top, scanning the area.

We cross a small road littered with trash and empty beer cans. When I was little, Hillcrest Park was a cool hippie hangout. But by the mid-eighties, druggies hung out in beat-up Buicks, the playground equipment was splintery, and dirty magazines were wadded up in the bushes.

"Keep your eyes peeled," Dad says with a chuckle, seeming unfazed. "Don't step on any used needles."

I feel a growing anxiety. I can't imagine why Dad wants this park to be our family meeting spot—Mom doesn't even let us play here anymore.

We walk up another smaller incline and come across an old abandoned picnic area at the top of the hill. The tables are covered in graffiti, and the public barbecues are rusted out. We stand at the edge of the hill and survey the land below.

The tall eucalyptus and palm trees muffle the traffic noise drifting up from Harbor Boulevard. And though the late afternoon light is thick with smog, I can still see Thrifty Drug Store where, after tent meetings, Dad takes us to get ice-cream cones for ten cents a scoop.

Dad pushes his cowboy hat back on his head and opens his arms wide to the view. "This is the spot!" he announces. "This is where I want you to go if your mom and I get arrested by the Antichrist."

I glance around, trying to catch his enthusiasm. "But Dad, Mom doesn't let us come up here," I say.

"Well, you only come here if we get arrested. It's the perfect spot because nobody will suspect it. Look! It's totally deserted!"

"Dad, why can't we just stay with you? I don't mind getting arrested by the Antichrist."

"Wiz, I know you're ready to give your life for the Lord. But just in case we get separated, you need a safe place to hide until we can send someone to get you. And I also have a secret family password for you!"

"What is it?"

Dad lowers his voice and cups his mouth with one hand. "Mephibosheth."

"Mephibo-what?"

"Mephibo-*sheth*. It's a rare, biblical name. Nobody will guess it."

"Me-phib-o-sheth," I repeat.

"You got it!"

I stand with Dad at the top of the hill and think about the secret password. *Mephibosheth*. It is a great word. But I still feel uncertain about the rest of our plan.

The thing is, I absolutely believe Dad is right about the whole Antichrist thing. I fully expect to get Raptured or martyred. The only thing I'm not sure about is the sketchy logistics of this family meeting spot. Like most of Dad's far-fetched plans, this one is too abstract. I need concrete details—the kind of answers Mom is good at providing.

The difference between Mom and Dad is that while they both believe Jesus is returning soon, they approach it in different ways. Dad inspires everyone with his grandiose visions of saving the world, while Mom packs the cooler and clean underwear.

I look up at Dad, wondering how to express my concern about his escape plan without making it seem as though I am questioning *him*. Dad is a real stickler about my asking questions in the right tone of voice.

"Dad, would it be a sin to steal food while we're camping here?"

Dad ponders this for a moment and then allows that stealing during the Antichrist's reign is not a sin. "It's better to steal than take the mark of the Beast," he explains. "And don't forget, you can always find food in dumpsters—Hey, why are you crying, Wiz?"

I shake my head, embarrassed. Dad is so positive and upbeat about his plan—*Come on, Wiz! It's an adventure!*—that for a moment I've almost forgotten we are really preparing for the End of the World.

Dad pulls me into a hug and chuckles. "Now, Wiz, it's all gonna be okay. The Lord is gonna take care of us. We just gotta trust Him! You believe I'm only lookin' out for your best interests, right?"

I nod. Of course I believe that! I believe *everything* Dad says. I believe 1988 is The End. I believe my life will be over in a couple of years.

The End is near. It is really happening.

"Now, show me a happy face," Dad says.

I force a smile.

"Good girl. Now keep a brave face. We don't want anyone at home asking why you're crying."

As Dad drives us home, I silently ask Jesus to come into my heart—for the 8,364th time.

Spoiler alert: Jesus didn't return in 1988.

This was the first thing that didn't go as planned. But it didn't seem to bother Papa George. He simply shrugged it off and reminded us he'd never said *for sure* Jesus was returning in 1988, just that it was a good possibility. And then he went on to preach that we needed to stay ready anyway because maybe God wanted to save more souls before "the wrath that was to come."

The second thing that didn't go as planned was that I started having night terrors. I'd intended to hone my reconnaissance skills, double down on Rapture readiness, and bulk up our family food stockpile. But instead I started to hear footsteps outside my window at night and began to wet the bed. When I lost sight of Mom in the grocery store, I went into full-blown screaming fits—not because I feared kidnapping but because I thought the Rapture had happened and I'd been Left Behind. I developed chronic stomach pain and was perpetually constipated. I alternated between sucking my thumb and sucking down bottles of Pepto-Bismol.

My bedtime prayers started sounding like a reading from the book of Revelation as I "prayed against" potential apocalyptic events. "Please, no earthquakes, pestilence, or bloody moons, Lord! And please forgive me for saying the *s* word." (Fundamentalist lexicon: the "*s* word" is *shut up*.)

If I forgot a natural disaster, I'd start all over again and list them thoroughly one more time. Mom would sit at the edge of my bed, calmly stifling a yawn as I frantically searched my conscience for sin—known and unknown, accidental and purposeful, and any other tiny thing I might have forgotten, Lord!

She seemed unconcerned about my scrupulosity, breezily kissing my forehead and saying she'd see me in the morning.

"Not if the Rapture happens first!" I'd cry.

"Oh, Elizabeth, stop being so dramatic," she'd say.

Mom's reactions often confused me. She didn't seem worried at all about getting ready for the End of the World. She kept dodging my Rapture-related questions with noncommittal replies and even seemed vaguely amused when I told her about Dad's secret family meeting spot and password.

"Your father," she would say with a chuckle. "What *has* he been telling you?"

Her calm didn't ease my fears. I wanted *answers*. I wanted to *stockpile*.

My fears were only exacerbated when we watched a campy Christian horror flick called *A Thief in the Night*. It was about getting Left Behind at the Rapture and all the horrible things that happened on Earth afterward. I was so scared that I had nightmares for months. I mean, I didn't regularly watch television or movies, so *A Thief in the Night* seemed completely realistic. I had no way to contextualize or understand the movie, and since it was based on theology my dad fully believed, I basically went into full-scale meltdown.

I started hiding in weird places because I thought it would be a good idea to practice evasion tactics. After all, if the Rapture happened and I was Left Behind, I needed to be sure the Antichrist's police couldn't find me. So I smashed myself into the tiny crawlspace behind Mom's waterbed, climbed trees and stayed perched up there for hours, buried myself in the back of closets and refused to come out. I wrote desperate letters to my imaginary friend, Elenob. I discovered masturbating and, delighted by this instant pain relief, kept excusing myself from family dinners to run upstairs and grind against my bedpost.

One day, Mom found me hiding in her closet, sucking my thumb and repeatedly running her silk scarves through my fingers. "I've had enough of this," she declared. "I'm taking you to the allergist."

Allergies, of course, were the only acceptable explanation for my bizarre symptoms. In our brand of fundamentalism, people with anxiety issues were people with weak faith. For *true* Christians like us, there was no such thing as mental illness.

Mom avoided American pediatricians, claiming they were all beholden to big pharmaceutical companies. She toted me off to a series of holistic practitioners who tapped my wrists, pried open my eyelids, and diagnosed me as lactose intolerant.

Mom found a Chinese herbalist named Dr. Vong, who'd reportedly cured cancer patients using nothing more than raw herbs slow-cooked in a Crock-Pot. Mom thought this was absolutely fabulous and a real answer to our prayers. Dr. Vong prescribed all kinds of tinctures, herbs, and mineral supplements to cure my "allergies." And although his foul-tasting herbal brews once cured me of bronchitis (while also giving me exploding-stars hallucinations), none of his alternative therapies ever cured me of Left Behind-itis.

As a last resort, Mom took me to a traditional Western pediatrician who declared I was perfectly healthy—which made Dad proclaim that my real sickness was Melodrama.

Then again, it was tough for doctors to accurately assess my emotional state since my parents weren't exactly honest with them. Mom would lay off the spankings for a few days and wait to take me to the doctor until the welts and marks had faded. Whenever a doctor asked about my home life, Dad found euphemistic ways of describing it. "We have several college students renting rooms from us," he would say.

"We have friends from out of state staying with us until they find their own place," Mom would add.

The truth was that my parents ran a strict missionary training home, and we had anywhere from six to ten people living with us at all times. Living in my home was sort of like living in a Christian commune—except with way more PMS and apocalypse stockpiling.

Chapter 3

Christian Commune

I n our home, privacy didn't exist. In fact, people who were serious about being Christians in The Assembly were strongly encouraged to give up their "worldly independence" and live communally in training homes. Zero privacy was an important part of being devout in The Assembly. This was how we prepared ourselves for the End of the World.

My parents ran a sisters' home; we always had six single women living with us and sometimes a whole other family. On any given day, people were coming and going, holding Bible studies, finding Jesus, making meals, doing chores, crying, laughing, getting engaged, and having babies. When a newly married couple moved into the bedroom next to mine, I asked Mom why I wasn't allowed to jump on my bed when they were allowed to jump on theirs every single night.

New converts were especially attracted to our communal way of life. They showed up on our doorstep full of dreams and ideals, ready to live their lives completely sold-out for Jesus. We had your garden-variety anorexics, fun-loving sorority girls, and hyperspiritual holy rollers who spent hours weeping into their Bibles. Occasionally we'd get a failed actress or musician fleeing a life of sin and debauchery for our simple life of Bible study and no makeup.

Living in a training home meant that in exchange for receiving free spiritual training from my parents, housemates cooked meals, cleaned the house, and baby-sat me. They also gave away their right to privacy, free time, and anything my parents deemed unfit for their spiritual growth. Before a woman moved in, Mom went through her entire wardrobe to ensure all the clothing was modest.

In our home, nothing was your own, including the bathroom. You did your private business while other women walked in and out. You picked the pubic hair out of the soap before lathering up. Even your period was not your own—your menstrual cycle synced up with all the other women's, a fact that often prompted Dad to remark that *he* was the victim of the PMS.

Despite these inconveniences, most people thought living in our training home was a privilege—probably because Dad kept saying so. Either way, people kept lining up to live with us. Mom managed everything by running our training home on a tight schedule.

At six thirty in the morning a bell rang, summoning everyone to prayer and Scripture reading in the living room. At seven o'clock we sat down for a communal family breakfast. Attendance at weeknight dinners was mandatory, as was attendance at all weekly church meetings. A cooking schedule was posted on the refrigerator, and each housemate received an assigned laundry day. Mom drew up a huge chart listing daily and weekly "stewardships," such as dusting, vacuuming, and bathroom cleaning.

To help her run the household, Mom appointed a Head Steward who made sure everyone completed her daily and weekly stewardships. When housemates neglected their duties, overslept, or missed meetings, the Head Steward doled out consequences, usually in fifteen-minute increments of extra work.

Additionally, the Head Steward was responsible for overseeing the spiritual health of each housemate and reporting back to Mom and Dad. If a housemate expressed a bad attitude, quarreled, or wasn't reading her

Bible daily, she was called into a private meeting with Mom and Dad to deal with her issues. Mom said an important part of missionary training was learning to live peaceably and cooperatively with other people.

And although our home was primarily directed toward missionary preparation, we often took in stray people, displaced families, traveling preachers, and the occasional random stranger. So many different people streamed through our home that it was common to show up for dinner and find new faces at the table.

On the one hand, it was fun to meet all kinds of people. On the other hand, it sucked to be awakened at three in the morning by the resident junkie yelling for her Percocet! Vicodin! *Get me my Phenergan!*

Being raised in this insular, highly regulated, hierarchical environment was sort of like growing up in a mob family. Except instead of killing people if they stopped cooperating, we just excommunicated them from our training homes. Religious fervor was all I knew, so my holy mob family felt normal. Didn't everybody's family have secret passwords, food stockpiles, and escape plans for surviving in a post-Rapture world? Didn't everybody confess her sins fifty times a day?

Sister Kathleen arrives on our doorstep carrying her guitar. She is wearing hot-pink lipstick and black leg warmers. Her bright blue eyes are lined in dark kohl.

"Call me Kat!" she announces, sweeping into the living room and doing a little spin in front of everyone. We all stare. Kat is tall and slender with a glowing mane of curly blond hair.

"I believe your name is Kathleen?" Mom asks calmly, standing and extending her hand.

Kat/Kathleen drops her guitar and flings her arms around Mom's neck. "Oh, I need to hug you! I'm so excited to be here! Thank you so much for welcoming me into your lovely home!"

I stare at Kathleen as if she's some kind of magical creature from the outside world. How has a woman like this landed in our strict missionary training home?

"We're just about ready to start our house meeting, Kathleen," Mom says. "Please sit down and make yourself comfortable. I'll introduce you to every—"

"Oh, may I just sing one song?" Kathleen interrupts. "By way of introduction?"

Mom's eyes widen. She is not accustomed to being interrupted. "Well, I suppose—"

"Oh, thank you!"

Kathleen pops open her guitar case, pulls out her guitar, and settles herself on the edge of a chair. She sticks a guitar pick in her mouth while she tunes the strings, eyes closed. Then her blue eyes spring open, and she smiles at all of us.

"I used to want to be a famous opera singer," she says, strumming her guitar while talking. "But then I gave my heart to Jesus, and now I just want Him to use my voice for *His* glory!"

Kathleen's guitar comes alive under her fingers, and she shakes back her blond curls, tilting her chin to the ceiling. "I've got a river of life flowing out of me! Makes the lame to walk and the blind to see! Spring up, oh well! Splish splash!"

I am spellbound. Kathleen has a sweetly raspy voice, and her body sways to the rhythm. I glance at Mom who is smiling but only politely. Kathleen finishes her song and looks around expectantly. Nobody claps. We never applaud for any performance because Dad says that brings glory to man and not to God.

"Thank you for sharing that with us," Mom finally says. "Now, it's time for us to share with you what it means to live in our training home."

"Oh yes! I so want to learn!" Kathleen says. She quickly puts away her guitar and snuggles in next to the other sisters on the couch as if they are all immediate best friends.

Later that night, as Mom brushes the tangles out of my hair, she tells Dad about Sister Kathleen. Dad rarely attends our house meetings because he is usually busy preparing sermons, answering phone calls, praying for people, and teaching younger men how to read their Bibles.

"My goodness, you should see Kathleen's clothes." Mom sighs. "It's just a slew of short skirts and tight jeans. I'm going to have to purge her whole wardrobe. Almost everything she owns is immodest."

"Well, at least she seems willing to learn," Dad remarks. He is stretched out on the bed wearing his mukluk slippers and flipping through a sailboat magazine.

"Yes, she has an eager spirit," Mom agrees. "But she's just so…worldly. I'm glad you didn't see her singing tonight. The way she moves her body and shakes her head is overtly sexual!"

"What does 'overtly sexual' mean?" I ask, piping up. Mom taps the back of my head with the brush and says, "Shh."

"We can't let her perform at an Assembly outreach until she cuts that out," Dad says. "The last thing I need is a bunch of guys showing up for Wednesday night Bible study because they saw Kathleen at a tent meeting."

Mom and Dad both laugh at this. I don't understand why that is funny so I stay quiet. The tangles are all smoothed out, but sometimes I just like Mom to run the brush through my hair over and over.

"I think I'll have her come to Cornerstone Academy and sing for the kids," Mom says. "There's no place for immodesty or self-glory when you're singing for children."

"Good idea, sweetheart! If Kathleen truly wants to use her gift for the Lord, then she shouldn't complain if the Lord asks her to sing for kids."

"Exactly right."

"How would you like that, Wiz?" Dad asks me. "Would you like Sister Kathleen to come sing at school?"

"That would be really fun!" I exclaim. "I like Sister Kathleen! She's the prettiest sister who has ever lived with us!"

Mom *tsks* and shakes her head. "My, my, Elizabeth. That's rather vain, don't you think? The Bible says man looks on the outward appearance but God looks on the heart. Sister Kathleen might be pretty on the outside, but what is the Lord *really* interested in?"

Mom glances at Dad as if remembering something. "And another thing I'll have to deal with is Kathleen's makeup and earrings. Did you see those huge hoops she was wearing?"

"Those definitely have to go," Dad says. "No pierced earrings in this house!"

Mom sighs again. "The gaudy nail polish has to go too. Oh boy. This is going to be a lot of work."

"Now, sweetheart, don't do everything by yourself. The Lord has called you to teach at Cornerstone Academy. Can't you assign the Head Steward to train Kathleen for the next couple of weeks?"

"Yes, I've assigned Sister Nancy to the job, but I have a feeling Sister Kathleen is going to be quite the handful. Nancy will probably need help breaking her in."

"Well, living in our home is a privilege, not a right. If Sister Kathleen doesn't respond to the training with humility, she is more than welcome to move out," Dad says.

"That's true," Mom replies. "Okay, Elizabeth, I'm done with your hair. Go get in bed, and I'll be in momentarily to pray with you."

I leave the bedroom, closing the door very quietly as Mom taught me. I walk down the hall feeling sad. I know Mom is right about Sister Kathleen. She is very worldly. But there is something so special about her too. Something fresh. Something carefree. Sister Kathleen doesn't seem like the type who spends hours reading her Bible or charting out her sin issues. She seems like the type who would maybe climb trees with me.

I can't help wondering how long she'll last.

I stand in the hallway and peek through the half-open door. Sister Kathleen is kneeling by her bed, crying. Her Bible and journal lie open on the bed. I tap on the door. "Sister Kathleen?"

She jumps. "Yes? Come in!"

I push open the door.

"Oh, hi, Elizabeth." Sister Kathleen looks relieved. "I thought maybe you were the Head Steward."

"Can I come in?"

"Yes, of course, sweetheart."

I climb up on Sister Kathleen's bed while she checks her face in a small mirror hanging over her dresser. "I just can't seem to stop crying today," she says, laughing a little at herself.

"Why are you sad?"

"Oh, I'm sure I'll feel better soon. I'm just learning how to die to self."

"But why were you crying?"

Sister Kathleen closes her Bible and notebook. She places them on top of her nightstand. She blows her nose and then looks at me intently. "Elizabeth, you are so blessed to have parents who are raising you in the nurture and admonition of the Lord. I didn't have that growing up."

"Did you get spanked?" I ask.

"No, never," she says. "And now, as an adult, it's very hard for me to learn how to obey. I'm…I'm trying very hard, but…but I keep messing up." Sister Kathleen's eyes are welling up with tears again. She pats them with the tissue.

"What happened? Did you get in trouble with the Head Steward?"

Sister Kathleen nods.

"What did you do?"

"I got dinner on the table ten minutes late. And I forgot to do my daily stewardships."

"So you got a big consequence?"

Sister Kathleen nods again. "But I shouldn't be telling you all this," she says, standing up. She pulls her purse off her dresser and starts scrounging through it. "Why did you come see me anyway?"

I shrug. "I just wanted to hang out with you."

Kathleen looks up from her purse. "Really?"

"Yeah! I like you!" I say.

Kathleen pulls a small pot of lip balm from her purse. She unscrews the lid and dabs some on her lips. "Want a little?" she asks.

I nod eagerly but then stop myself. "Does it have color in it? Mom says I can't wear anything with color."

"Don't worry. It's just Carmex."

"Oh, okay."

Kathleen gently pats the balm on my mouth. "You have pretty lips. When you grow up, you're going to be a knockout."

"What's a 'knockout'?"

Kathleen throws back her head and laughs. I love Sister Kathleen's laugh. It is loud and open. She doesn't try to hold it back like so many other sisters do. I want her to stay with us forever.

"I wish you were coming with us on the missionary and training team!" I blurt. "I really wanted you to come with us. I don't like it that Dad is making you stay here."

Sister Kathleen stops laughing. She sits next to me on the bed and places an arm around my shoulder. "I really wanted to go too. But…well, your dad doesn't think I'm ready yet. I still have a lot to learn."

"Are you still worldly?" I ask.

Sister Kathleen doesn't reply. She lies back on the bed and stares at the ceiling. She is quiet for such a long time I think maybe she hasn't heard my question. Finally, Sister Kathleen sighs deeply and rolls over to face me. "I don't know, Elizabeth," she says softly. "I don't know anything anymore."

She looks so sorrowful I don't know what to say. I've seen this before. Sometimes when sisters who lived with us got really depressed, they left. They just packed up their things and disappeared without so much as a good-bye. I don't want this to happen to Sister Kathleen. I have an idea for cheering her up. "Can you practice your opera with me?" I ask. "You know, like how we used to? I'll hold the sheet music, and you sing for me?"

Sister Kathleen shakes her head. "I gave up opera," she says. "I'm not studying it anymore."

"But you're still singing, right?"

"I still love singing. But your grandmother Betty said maybe the Lord is asking me to give that up too."

"But why?"

"Elizabeth, I'm sorry, sweetheart. I shouldn't be telling you all this. I could get in trouble again."

"I won't tell anyone!"

"I know. But listen to me. You have good Christian parents who love you and only want God's best for you. For all of us."

I nod silently. "God's best." Dad has been talking and preaching about this a lot recently. He says God's best isn't about making us happy; it is about making us holy. We can miss out on God's best if we don't follow God's will for our lives. Dad says we will know God's will by obeying those in authority over us. So we are supposed to honor those who "stand for God's best" in our lives.

Maybe by telling her to give up music, Grandma Betty is trying to "stand for God's best" in Sister Kathleen's life. Maybe by spanking me so much, my parents are doing the same thing in my life.

God doesn't want me to be happy, I remember. *He wants me to be holy.*

Eventually Sister Kathleen was sent to live on a farm in the Midwest. Grandma Betty said living with a simple Assembly family was exactly the kind of spiritual training Sister Kathleen needed in order to purge her "worldly Hollywood dreams" from her soul.

Years later, Mom told me Sister Kathleen hadn't lasted very long in the Midwest.

"Poor thing," Mom said. "I was always afraid she'd fall away. The World had such a strong pull on her heart."

Sister Kathleen had "left the Lord"—which really meant she'd left The Assembly. I hope she's singing Verdi somewhere.

Chapter 4

Grand Masters of My Destiny

Grandma Betty was on her deathbed. Then again, she'd been dying ever since I could remember.

Papa George said she'd been healed of cancer after he fasted and prayed for her. But Grandma Betty said her recovery was thanks to an all-natural diet and coffee enemas. Years later she still tottered on death's doorstep, her enfeebled state necessitating a bevy of personal assistants who cooked, cleaned, and brewed gallons of coffee in giant soup pots. Whenever I used Grandma's bathroom, I avoided looking at her enema bag. It made me nauseous.

Each year on my birthday, Grandma Betty summoned me to her bedroom for an appointment. I would sit stiffly on the edge of her blue-flowered love seat while she interrogated me. For being deathly frail, Grandma sure had plenty of energy for meddling in everyone's business. How was my walk with the Lord? Was I reading my Bible daily and praying? Was I confessing my sins? Was I ready for Jesus's return? And the big one: *Are you redeeming the time?*

"Redeeming the time" meant living in a state of constant readiness because, as Papa George often warned us, "Ooohhh, the shame of it all!" if Jesus returned and we were listening to secular music or something.

Life wasn't about living; it was about preparing for Eternity. Things like having fun, listening to music, hanging out with friends, or just being a kid were a waste of precious time. As I mentioned, my parents never saved for my college education or even their own retirement because they were preparing for things of higher, eternal value, such as dying for the Lord.

Of course, these were the kinds of things everyone in The Assembly obsessed over. All this emphasis on "redeeming the time" meant I'd been preparing for my death since the day I was born. My future was clear: either I'd prove myself worthy of being Raptured, or I'd die during the Antichrist's global takeover.

On my sixth birthday, Grandma Betty summons me to her home for my usual interrogation. But this time is different. After the barrage of deeply personal questions, Grandma announces she has a special gift for me.

"Elizabeth, can you tell me why birthdays are important?" she asks, staring at her hands folded neatly in her lap.

For a moment, I panic. Grandma's questions are notoriously tricky. They only *seem* to have obvious answers. Once, when she'd asked why I still sucked my thumb, I'd answered that it made me feel good. Grandma said that wasn't the real reason. She said I was rebellious (because Mom had been trying to break me of the habit for years) and self-indulgent (because sucking my thumb meant I relied on physical comfort instead of finding my comfort in the Lord).

At the time, I had no idea why sucking my thumb was selfish, but as I grew up, I realized that, in The Assembly, *anything* that made me feel good was probably sinful.

Grandma looks up from her hands. "Well?"

"I...I...birthdays are important because..." I cast around in my mind, trying to find a pleasing answer. "Because it's another year to serve the Lord!"

Grandma raises a suspicious eyebrow at me. "I *see.*"

Wrong answer! Wrong answer! I have a sudden urge to chew on my hair. Instead, I pull my homemade dress over my thumb and hide it. My thumb is red and raw from all my earnest sucking.

Although I never told Grandma Betty, thumb sucking is the least of my soothing mechanisms. I've developed a whole slew of odd little tics. I suck my hair into sticky daggers and stick them in my ears. I fold my pillowcase into a tight point and poke it in the corner of my eye. I hide in Mom's closet and drag her scarves through my fingers until my skin is raw.

And now, having just given Grandma a wrong answer, I feel my anxiety rise. I fear she has x-ray vision and can see all my hidden sins.

Giving me an unflinching stare from her icy-blue eyes, Grandma uses her foot to push a small brown suitcase toward me. "So presents aren't important on birthdays?" she asks.

"Oh! Yes!" I chirp, grateful she is giving me a second chance. "I love presents!"

Grandma juts her head at the suitcase, and I slide off the love seat to pick it up. A bright spark of hope flickers inside me. Is there a doll inside? Or maybe scratch 'n' sniff stickers? I unzip the suitcase.

It is empty. I look up at Grandma, confused.

"Stand up, Elizabeth," Grandma orders.

I stand, clasping the little brown suitcase by my side. Grandma looks me up and down and then places her hands on my shoulders. "Straighten your shoulders," she says. "Your middle name is Esther, so you should have the posture and bearing of a queen."

I pull up straight and try to swallow my disappointment about the empty suitcase.

"Very good. You look like an obedient little missionary," she says.

I nod.

"Did you know that God has called the Geftakys family to serve Him?"

I nod.

"That's why I bought you a suitcase for your birthday. You can use it for your family missionary trips this summer."

"Thank you, Grandma, for this birthday present," I say, remembering Mom's stern reminder that I say thank you no matter what I get.

"George!" Grandma Betty calls. "George! Come see your granddaughter!"

Papa George comes bursting into the room. He is a hurricane force of a man, six feet tall with a broad face, thick lips, and a high forehead. He is a fastidious dresser and slaps on enough aftershave to knock out an elephant. I turn to face him, and he throws open his arms. "Come give Papa a kiss!" he roars.

I take two steps toward him, and he reaches down, swoops me up in his arms, and crushes me against his sweaty cheek. Still holding me high, he parades me out of the bedroom and into his study.

"Isn't she wonderful? Isn't she grand?" he demands of his secretary, and she murmurs yes, indeed, amen.

"It's her birthday today!" Papa booms, as if he is making one of his huge, biblical pronouncements. "What gift shall we render to such a one as this?"

Papa's secretary, as if on cue, scurries out from behind her little desk, carrying a wrapped gift. Papa crashes down in his massive desk chair, and I take my place on a straight-backed seat nearby.

"Elizabeth Esther Geftakys!" he thunders, his voice at full preaching volume. "This gift I'm about to give you is symbolic of the great plan God has for your life! From before the foundations of the world, God knew you! And He knit you together in your mother's womb! He endowed you with gifts and purpose, hallelujah!"

Papa always talks like this—yelling just as loudly in church as he does in restaurants, airports, or bookstores. Wherever he goes, people stop to stare or shake their heads in annoyance. He is charismatic, mysterious, brilliant, and mercurial—as equally prone to outbursts of spiritual insight as he is to outbursts of scathing temper. To me, he is God.

Papa George hands me the gift and leans forward, watching intently. "Don't rip the paper!" he warns. "Save it and give it to your mother. Maybe she can use it for another gift."

I carefully unwrap the present. In Papa George and Grandma Betty's view, childish stuff like ripping open presents is intolerable. Childhood is a time of serious preparation for Christian service and the End Times.

I finally get the wrapping paper off the present and gently open the cardboard box. It isn't a toy. It isn't anything I need or even want at age six. It's a pair of bookends.

I pull one out of the box. A small world globe, set in a longitudinal frame, spins slowly when I touch it. I look up at Papa George, and he has a knowing smile on his face.

"I've seen you eyeing that one," he explains, pointing at the world globe he keeps in a corner of his study.

I am surprised. It is true that I've been fascinated by his globe and that on a few special occasions he's let me examine it, but I am taken aback that he remembered. Papa George, I realize, is always watching.

"These bookends serve a special purpose," Papa George continues. "They should remind you that God has called the Geftakys family to preach the gospel across the world."

"Thank you, Papa," I say.

"That's my *darling*!" he crows. "Now, give your ol' Papa a big smooch on the cheek and never forget what it means to be a Geftakys!"

I go home that day with the bookends tucked into the little brown suitcase.

My destiny has been chosen for me. I am to be an obedient little missionary, saving as many souls as possible before the End of the World.

Chapter 5

Bible Boot Camp

The little brown suitcase went with me to Bible camp.

This was not your crafting, canoeing, sing-around-the-campfire summer camp. No, no. We believed in *edification*. We learned good character by digging trenches in the rain, reading the Bible for hours, and camping in tents. Assembly Bible camp was more like a boot camp for holiness.

Worldly children cared about having fun and being entertained, but we, the Children of the Lord, cared only about becoming like Jesus. Which, of course, meant suffering. And maybe a scourging or two.

Before camp, Mom gave the counselors a list of my character defects, expecting a full report on my spiritual progress. Assembly adults were permitted to spank children because thoroughly breaking a child's will required the participation of *all* Assembly members. It was a silent pact of complicity, and everyone was in on it.

This is the chief marker of cultish fundamentalism: everyone must obey. Fundamentalism isn't so much about belief as it is about behavior. Mainly, fundamentalism is about sameness. We spoke Assembly, we lived Assembly, we spanked our kids Assembly. Everything was controlled. Anything different required prior approval.

And when I say everything was controlled, I mean literally right down to when and where I relieved myself.

The year I take the little brown suitcase to camp is the year we get rained out and Brother Larry, our camp leader, digs a trench and tells us to use it as our toilet.

But I can't do it. Long after all the other "good kids" have finished their business, I remain squatted over the muddy trench unable to relax long enough to go.

My counselor, Sister Martha, stomps over to me and digs her fists into her waist. "I'm gonna make you squat here until you choose to obey," she says.

I hitch my dress above my waist and try again. It is still raining, and the drops trickle down my neck.

But I can't go. I don't know what is wrong with me. Ever since I arrived in the mountains, my stomach has clenched up solid. Mom and Dad are at a conference in Colorado, and I am stuck up at Bible camp with an uncooperative colon.

Sister Martha says I should be able to squat and poop like all the other obedient children at Bible camp. But clearly, I am choosing to be in rebellion, which is "as the sin of witchcraft," 1 Samuel 15:23. My rebellion is causing her to stand out here in the rain.

"Elizabeth, for a preacher's daughter, you sure set a poor example," she says.

It has rained for two days straight, flooding the camp bathrooms. The park rangers close the bathrooms and say maybe we should go home. But Brother Larry and Sister Martha say Christians don't quit.

"Brother Larry has been kind enough to dig this trench for us," Sister Martha says. "The least you can do is go in it."

I continue squatting over the muddy trench, my naked bottom exposed to the rain and wind. I close my eyes and try to relax. *Lord Jesus, please help me poop.* Nothing happens. I open my eyes. Sister Martha is in my face, her beady eyes bulging behind thick glasses.

"If you don't go right now, I'm going to spank you," she hisses through clenched teeth.

A sudden, frightened spurt of urine runs between my legs and into the mud. Sister Martha sees it and shakes her head. "That's it? That's *all* you can do?"

I can't talk. My tongue, like my colon, has frozen up. Sister Martha yanks my arm and marches me out of the trench, my dress still held above my waist. She hands me some toilet paper, and I wipe myself as she watches, her mouth twisted in disapproval.

"I won't spank you, Elizabeth," she says. "But I *am* sending you to bed without dinner."

We trudge back to camp, our heads bent against the rain. It is growing dark. All I can think about is burying myself in my sleeping bag and sucking my thumb.

Back at our campsite, the boys have dug a moat around our tent. The girls are piling our muddy suitcases and sleeping bags in the middle of the tent while the floor sloshes beneath their bare feet like a dirty waterbed.

"Come on, Wiz!" my cousin Rachel calls. "We're gonna march around our stuff like we're marching around the walls of Jericho!"

One of the older girls, Joy, flings her arms in the air and starts stomping around the sleeping-bag pile, singing at the top of her lungs, "We're marching to Zion, beautiful, beauuuutiful Zion!"

I watch Joy, giggling nervously. She's gotten in trouble every single day. She is loud. She talks back. She is given extra chores and sent to bed hungry. But her punishments seem only to make her more determined. She never cries. She sticks her chin in the air and announces she'll starve for a month! Starve her way into the Kingdom!

Slowly, we join Joy's march. We sing. We sing louder. And then we holler.

"Hallelujah!" Joy shouts.

"Amen!" we shout back.

Obviously, hollering isn't an approved camp activity. It smacks of fun. It smacks of entertainment. Until that moment, our sole source of entertainment has been singing Bible songs with Brother Larry. He's taught us songs about climbing Jacob's ladder-ladder and having mansions "just over the hilltop in that bright land where we'll never grow old." Like all the other adults in The Assembly, Brother Larry is excited about dying because this ol' world is not his home; he is just "passin' through."

As we march and sing, I'm terrified we'll get caught. But all the adults are outside, preoccupied with salvaging our rained-out camp. For one rare, shining moment, we kids are alone.

We keep up the revelry until suddenly Brother Larry pulls back the tent flap and pokes his head inside. We freeze midsong. We are sweaty, muddy, and guilty as sin.

Brother Larry's face registers shock. But when he starts talking, he sounds defeated. All the mansion-in-glory-land is gone from his voice. We are going home, he says. One of the boys has broken an ankle. "Pack your stuff and haul it out to the vans," Larry says and disappears.

We all stare at each other. I can't believe we aren't getting spanked or forced to eat more cold leftovers of Sister Martha's Pritikin diet food.

One of my friends, Eden, leans close. "We're escaping the gulag," she whispers.

I laugh.

We've been saved.

Chapter 6

Love Is Patient, Love Is Violent

I'm ten years old. Before my spanking, Mom tells me to sit on her bed while she draws a diagram of my sins. She says I must understand why I need this spanking. I am old enough now to calmly discuss my disobedience.

On a piece of notebook paper, she assigns each of my sins a "swat value." Being disobedient equals three swats. Lying about what I did equals four swats. Mom adds up my sins and circles the number seven with her pencil. "Do you believe you deserve this spanking?" she asks.

I can't talk because something is blocking my throat. I nod.

Mom nods at her bed. That is my cue. I know what is required. I pull down my culottes and underwear, stretch myself across her waterbed. I must not scream, I must not cry out loudly, or I will receive more swats. Some parents I know give their kids ten to fifteen swats per spanking. We are all spanked multiple times per day.

Mom takes her time. She pauses between each swat. She spanks me so hard it jars my whole body forward. I feel my jaw clamp shut, rattling my teeth. I focus on a tiny flower in the pattern of Mom's bedspread. I stare at it until I can feel myself disappearing into it, sending my mind far, far away.

After it is over, I pull up my underwear and have a quiet talk with Mom.

"You must always tell the truth," Mom says. "Even when it's difficult. Even if it means you might get in trouble. You must not lie because God desires truth in the inward parts."

"Yes, Mom."

She hugs and kisses me. I ask her to forgive me, and she says she does.

The next day when I look in the mirror, my bottom is bruised. It hurts to sit down. It hurts to walk. God desires truth in the inward parts, I remind myself. My parents spank me because the book of Proverbs says it will save my soul from hell. Even though Dad says I'm a Christian because I asked Jesus into my heart, the Bible says God chastens His children.

My parents hurt me because they love me.

In The Assembly, Grandma Betty taught parents to spank their children until the "will is broken." The idea was that if parents broke their children's will in infancy, the kids were primed to obey God for the rest of their lives. To achieve this, Assembly parents started spanking their children while they were still babies, just months old. My grandmother called this child-training.

Mom broke my will with a large, flat wooden paddle. On the handle, Mom had printed a Scripture verse in pretty calligraphic writing: "The rod and reproof give wisdom." Our paddle was so well used it had a crack down the middle. Eventually, Mom broke it over my literally callused bottom.

A huge part of my child-training meant sitting quietly on a small sleeping mat during every church meeting. Most of our weekday meetings were two hours long. But on Sundays we held morning and afternoon meetings, so I typically logged five hours on my mat. If I didn't sleep or play quietly on my mat, I was spanked.

Grandma Betty also taught mothers to apply a standard of behavior called "first-time obedience." This meant that a child's obedience could be measured by how quickly she acted upon her parent's command. Delayed obedience was disobedience. Issuing a command more than once was a sign of parental weakness.

To ensure children were thoroughly broken and fully mat-trained, Grandma Betty encouraged parents to set up obedience tests. Some parents did this by placing M&M'S around children's mats, intentionally tempting them to disobey and then spanking them when they touched the candy.

Grandma Betty encouraged my spankings because she said I was a strong-willed child with a rebellious streak. Children, Grandma said, were inherently wicked sinners. Hard, daily spankings were the only way to save my soul from hell.

An often misunderstood aspect of religiously motivated spanking is the idea that it's always done in anger. In fact, the truth is almost the exact opposite. In my experience—and the experience of many other children who were raised by parents who spanked them for religious reasons—a spanking session was carried out coolly, methodically, and with systematic precision. My parents never yelled or lashed out in a moment of anger. Rather, my mom referred to our spanking sessions as The Cycle of Discipline, and they included a conversation, confession, spanking, and reconciliatory hugs.

What I've come to understand is that all the holy intentions in the world can't save a child from the living hell that becomes his or her life in a household that views corporeal punishment as the alpha and omega of discipline. My mom held meetings where young moms gathered to learn how to correctly wield a spanking instrument. Sometimes when a child was particularly "rebellious," Mom would invite the mother over for a child-training session. I'll never forget sitting at the top of the stairs listening to toddlers get spanked over and over and over in the living room below.

I felt kinda guilty about it, but I was glad other kids were getting spanked hard too. I mean, if we were all getting spanked, it had to be okay, right?

"You must be understanding toward my brother," Dad explains as we drive to Uncle David's house. "He's got a terrible disease."

"But I don't like playing at Uncle David's house," I say. "He's scary."

"He's not scary!" Dad scoffs.

Everyone says the diabetes is to blame for Uncle David's rage. My uncle doesn't have a temper. He has *insulin reactions.* Uncle David doesn't beat my cousins. He *disciplines* them.

"Did he ever hit you?" I ask.

"When I was little, yeah," Dad says. "But I outgrew him pretty quick, and he stopped messing with me."

"Maybe Uncle David won't be home today," I say hopefully. Uncle David doesn't work a regular job because of his diabetes. Sometimes he is home tinkering on his black Pontiac GTO, and sometimes he disappears for days.

Papa George says Uncle David is preparing himself for church planting in central California. Grandma Betty says Uncle David requires more rest time than most people so we shouldn't question his daily schedule.

We pull up to my uncle's house, a single-story rental in Fullerton. The grass hasn't been cut in months, and huge oil stains show on the cracked cement driveway. The front door opens, and two of my cousins come running out of the house, barefoot. Aunt Grace appears in the doorway, balancing her baby girl on one hip.

The empty driveway means Uncle David is gone. I smile and open the van door. My cousins hop inside, all talking at once. "The chickens laid eggs! The grass is so tall it covers our heads! Mama says we can make a grass maze!" We tumble out of the van together, Rachel and Little David holding my hands.

"Bye, Wiz!" Dad calls as we disappear into the grass.

I turn and run back to him, then cling to his leg. "Will you get me before dinner? Before it gets dark?"

Dad pats my head. "I don't know what time Mom is picking you up. Remember, she's working hard on her master's degree so she can start a school and teach all you kids."

"But where are *you* going?" I ask, hugging his leg tighter.

"Wiz, come on. I already told you this."

"You have to preach?"

"Yes, at a campus Bible study in Los Angeles. I won't be back until late tonight. After you're in bed. So, be a good girl now and go—"

I interrupt him. "Can I tell you a secret?"

"Elizabeth, that's enough."

He knows I am stalling, inventing reasons to make him stay. He gives me one last hug, and I stick my thumb in my mouth. Dad gets in the van and backs out of the driveway, waving jauntily at us.

Aunt Grace pulls me against her and squeezes me. "Don't be scared, Little Wizard," she says. "I promise you'll have fun playing here."

She is right. The afternoon passes easily. We spend hours making paths through the towering grass, sprawling on the back deck, and coloring huge murals on butcher paper. Little David has recently recovered from a bout of Kawasaki disease, and because he is still weak, Rachel makes a bed for him in a little wagon. We pull him around the backyard, and he cackles at the stories we make up for him.

We have just moved inside to play dress up when Uncle David comes bursting through the front door, roaring for Aunt Grace. His face is pinched and red, and the veins stand out on his neck like ropes.

We scramble behind the couch. Uncle David is six feet tall, lean, and tightly muscled. His hair is close shaven, military style. He wears cowboy boots, slim-cut jeans, and black mirrored aviator sunglasses. He pounds across the wood floor and blazes into the kitchen.

Suddenly, plates start crashing. Aunt Grace screams.

"It's okay," Rachel whispers. "He's just having an insulin reaction."

Little David motions at us. "We gotta hide," he says. We scurry into the kids' room and hide under Rachel's bed.

I glance over at Little David, who makes a silly face. We giggle at him, and he bugs out his eyes like a dying fish. I try to focus on him instead of Aunt Grace's screaming in the kitchen, but I can't help wondering if Uncle David will beat us next. Rachel has shown me the marks on her bottom, and I know Uncle David's spankings are a lot harder than the ones I get at home.

"Sometimes Mama calms him down by getting into bed with him," Rachel whispers.

"Why?" I ask.

Rachel shrugs. "Mama calls it 'making babies.'"

I don't know what that means, but I'm not about to let on, so I just nod. "Oh."

A door slams. It is quiet.

We wait a few minutes and then creep out from under the bed. We tiptoe to the kitchen. Aunt Grace is calmly sipping coffee at the table. Her eyes are red from crying, but when she sees us, she smiles brightly. "I just had a great idea! We should go outside and hunt for those chicken eggs! Who wants breakfast for dinner?"

We all say that sounds like fun. Aunt Grace leads us outside, quietly sliding the glass door shut behind us.

"Uncle David is very, very sick, and we must let him rest," she whispers to me. "The Lord has given him a heavy cross to bear."

Aunt Grace seems so happy that I figure maybe she doesn't mind Uncle David's outbursts. Papa George always says that we each have our own cross to bear. Uncle David has to bear his diabetes, and Aunt Grace has to bear Uncle David's insulin reactions.

"God chose the Geftakys family to do a great work for Him," Aunt Grace says as she breaks eggs into the frying pan. "We don't question the work of the Lord, do we?"

"No, we don't!" answers Rachel. "Working for the Lord is a *privilege,* right, Mama?"

Aunt Grace nods and silently stirs the eggs. We sit at the table, patiently waiting. Baby Becca bangs her spoon on her highchair. I glance at the closed bedroom door, desperately hoping Uncle David will stay in there until Mom comes to get me.

"Do we question the Lord's servants?" Aunt Grace asks, setting plates of scrambled eggs in front of us.

We soberly shake our heads. Anyone who gets in the way of God's servants is getting in the way of God. We bear our crosses and stay out of God's way.

I comfort myself by humming a little tune: "Soon and very soon we are going to see the King." Jesus can return any minute, but He'll probably come in 1988. That's what Papa George always says. I count to 1988 on my fingers. I'll be eleven in 1988. Surely I can bear my cross until then.

Keep myself pure, stay out of God's way, and bear my cross. *Soon and very soon.*

We eat our eggs without salt.

Chapter 7

School at the End of the World

Attending public school was out of the question. Dad called public school a "bastion of the State" and said its primary purpose was government indoctrination. Dad wanted us, as children of God, raised in the nurture and admonition of the Lord. So Mom opened her own school—essentially a glorified home school—and called it Cornerstone Academy.

We didn't have a proper building, so we moved around a lot. Mom held classes in parks, community centers, and the YMCA. Eventually we rented Sunday school classrooms at a local Baptist church.

Bible-based school or not, the kids on the playground soon created a hierarchy of power. At the top of the heap was a fierce tangle of Mexican kids whose parents had joined The Assembly. As the principal's daughter, a preacher's kid, and the eldest granddaughter of The Assembly's founding preacher, I was an obvious target.

I came to believe that *mi familia* meant "we can kill ya." Especially when it came to dodge ball.

Those boys launched the balls like rockets, blasting my legs out from underneath me and landing me face first on the blacktop. They called me "Gringa," "Holy Roller," "Whitey," "Fatty," "Little Princess," and "Goody Two-Shoes" and said they felt sorry for the guy who had to marry me.

They laughed at my frizzy hair and buckteeth. They said my skin was white because God didn't bake me long enough.

I quickly learned that tattling resulted only in being punished later, usually during an "accident" at recess. I got "accidentally" smashed in the mouth during dodge ball, pushed off the swings, and bounced off the teetertotter. *"No, Mrs. Principal, I didn't push your daughter off the swings. She fell off! Honest!"*

One day I come home with a huge swelling on my head. I am feeling dizzy and nauseous. One of the Mexican boys, Gabriel, had "accidentally" dropped a large wooden construction block on my head. He claimed he hadn't seen me sitting there.

Dad sees me stagger past his study and calls me in. He gently parts my matted hair and examines the knot. "Well," he says, "at least it's not bleeding anymore. I don't know why those kids don't like you, but I don't ever want you hitting them back."

I know why the Mexican kids don't like me because they've made that perfectly clear: I am white, I am weak, and I am the principal's daughter.

"I really want them to like me," I tell Dad. "Sometimes if I let them hurt me in dodge ball, they're really nice the rest of the day. Maybe I have to let people hit me so they can like me, right? Sometimes I just have to let them pinch me under the table and not tattle, right?"

Dad swivels in his chair and props up his feet on the desk. "Well, Elizabeth, Jesus tells us never to return evil for evil. Instead of trying to be their friend, why don't you find ways to serve them?"

"But how can I serve them when they don't even want me near them? They say I'm disgusting!"

Dad pokes my belly. "You are a little tubby."

"Dad, I'm being serious."

Dad sighs and pops his chair forward. I can tell I am beginning to tire him with my needs. He stands up and stretches, and when he starts talking again, he is using his pulpit voice. "Elizabeth! I got some good news for ya!"

"Okay."

"Fighting with fists is overrated. Any fool can throw a punch. And most do. But the real battles are won by fighting with your mind, your words, and your imagination. Use the gifts God gave you and fight back with better *ideas*."

I stand very still, absorbing this. I feel the painful throbbing in my head, but I also feel a new, strange thrill in my heart. *Fight back with better ideas.* I've never heard that before. It excites me. "I like that," I say.

"See, Wiz? Stick with me and you'll do okay. Now, go put some ice on that bump before it explodes."

"But, Dad?"

"What?"

"What if a robber broke into our house? Would you hit him?"

"No, no, I wouldn't. I'd try to restrain him, but I wouldn't lay my hands on him. I'm a pacifist, see."

"Even if the robber was trying to hurt me, you wouldn't hit him?"

"No, but I'd definitely be saying some prayers, Wiz; you can count on that. Now don't make me say it again: go ice your head."

I wander to the kitchen feeling confused. Apparently, being a pacifist means hitting your kid to save her soul from hell but *not* hitting an intruder to save her life.

"I just don't understand this," Miss Jones says, peering at my paper. "Your resting heart rate simply can't be over a hundred beats per minute. That's way too high."

I shrug. "I don't know why it's like that. I did this science experiment exactly the way you told me to."

Miss Jones squints at me. "But this doesn't make sense. The only way your heart rate would be this high is if you were scared out of your mind." She chuckles lightly. "Elizabeth, what are you scared of?"

I don't answer. I'm not about to tell her I am scared every single day of my life. Even at this age I know admitting fear is the same as admitting weak faith. I know better than to say out loud I am a bad Christian.

Next to me, my friend Eden holds up her paper. "My heart rate is high too," she says.

Miss Jones takes Eden's paper and examines it. "This doesn't make sense! Are you girls doing the experiment properly?"

"Yes, Miss Jones," Eden replies.

I glance at her. Eden is gnawing on her nails again, biting them down to the quick. She gets smashed in dodge ball too. And she is brilliant, which means the Mexican kids taunt her for using big words and reading "boring" books by Charles Dickens.

"Well, I want you girls to take your pulse again," Miss Jones says. "But this time, sit very still for a few minutes before you do it, okay?"

We nod obediently and go back to our table.

We do the experiment over and over, but our heart rates are always high. I feel anxious about this because I hate getting the "wrong answer." I am tempted to write a smaller number just to get the experiment *right*. In the end, Miss Jones accepts our results, but the mystery of our rapidly beating little hearts isn't questioned.

When Mom rings the bell for recess, I start asking if I can stay inside and read books. When she says no, I hide in the bathroom.

And I start doing other things too. I open and close doors a certain way, lock and unlock doors several times "just to be sure," touch certain spots on the wall as I pass, repetitively wash my hands.

I also start spanking my cat.

Yeah. I spank Frisky.

At the time, I don't know why I am doing it. I tell myself that I am just trying to "teach Frisky a lesson" about not running out into the street. But somehow, hitting Frisky makes me feel better. I get spanked every day at home and bullied every day at school. Spanking Frisky is my secret revenge.

Sometimes if I catch Frisky near the edge of the property, I lock him in the dark storage shed where we keep our trash cans. I've seen Dad do this when he discovered Frisky's paw prints all over the hood of his car. I tell myself that I'm not as bad as Dad because I only calmly spank the cat after a time-out in the shed, whereas Dad is prone to drop-kicking Frisky across the driveway.

Eventually, Frisky starts running away whenever he sees me coming. In fact, Frisky starts running whenever *anyone* goes near him. I don't understand it. *Doesn't Frisky realize I am only trying to help him?*

Not long after, Frisky goes missing. When we talk about it at dinner, Dad starts chuckling. He'd seen Frisky on his way home earlier that day. Oh yes, he said, the cat "has become road carpet."

"What does that mean?" I ask.

I look at Mom's face. She is shaking her head at Dad. Nobody speaks.

"Frisky's *dead*?" I croak.

Dad shrugs. "That's what he gets for running out into the street."

I start crying, and Mom excuses me from the table.

I cry myself to sleep that night. A heavy weight of guilt feels as if it might crush my chest. I hate how mean Dad was to Frisky; I hate how mean kids are to me; I hate how mean I was to Frisky.

I hate that I am becoming what I hate.

As leaders in The Assembly, my parents wanted to avoid the appearance of favoritism, so they refrained from intervening on my behalf. I was simply expected to turn the other cheek because our family was supposed to set a good example. The end result, however, was that I felt this obligation to tolerate the Mexican kids' abusive treatment in order to preserve my standing as a good pastor's daughter.

I took solace in knowing that The End was coming up quickly and that, because these kids were so mean, they'd definitely get Left Behind when the Rapture happened.

In fact, The End loomed so large that even the Mexican kids—usually supercool and unflappable—began talking about Papa George's predictions. During recess, we ate our lunches out of brown paper bags and discussed the inevitability of Something Big happening. We compared notes on which families were the most prepared and generally agreed that our lives would be over in a couple of years.

I wadded up my trash and wondered whether I should bother throwing it away—everything was going up in flames soon anyway. But since my personal Rapture readiness plan included a scrupulous attention to detail, I figured not littering would show God I was worthy of escaping the "wrath that was to come." Besides, Dad said he wanted to include me in his special, secret plans for outwitting the Antichrist. I didn't want to miss out on that by being lazy about litter.

I deposited my trash in the proper receptacle.

Chapter 8

Left Behind

The Rapture happened on an ordinary Saturday afternoon while I was napping.

Earlier that day, Mom had found me hiding under her desk. I tried to pretend that I wasn't *hiding* hiding. I was just...you know, praying. Meditating. Or something.

Mom tipped my face up to look at her. "You're tired and overwrought," she pronounced. "I can see it in your eyes. Go upstairs immediately and take a nap."

She couldn't have given me a better punishment. I especially liked taking naps when our communal home was bustling with people because it meant I wouldn't be alone if the Rapture happened.

On the day the Rapture happened, everyone was preparing for Sunday—what we called "All Day for God." From the safety of my bed, I heard the distant noises of flatware clanking in the kitchen, the phone ringing, the vacuum on the stairs.

Sister Nancy was ironing Dad's dress shirts right outside my bedroom door, and I was lulled to sleep by the hiss and creak of the old ironing board and iron. Just before I fell asleep, I drowsily said a prayer asking Jesus into my heart. One more time. Just to be safe.

The first time I asked Jesus into my heart I was four years old. One of the sisters who lived with us was reading her Bible, and she seemed so happy and peaceful that I wanted to copy her. I knelt next to her and asked Jesus to come into my heart. I felt something inside. It felt like a sigh of relief. It made me smile.

"Jesus is real!" I told Mom. "He's really real!"

I loved the feeling so much I started asking Jesus into my heart all the time. Once, when I was six, I lay prostrate on my bed and begged Jesus to save me and bring me safely into heaven. I felt the Jesus Sigh of relief again.

When I was eight and worrying about the Rapture, I asked Jesus into my heart every day. But I didn't feel the Jesus Sigh anymore.

Shortly after Dad laid out our survival plan, I grew more desperate. I hadn't felt the Jesus Sigh in a long time, and I wanted to make sure God still loved me. I wanted Him to know I still loved Him, still believed in Him. Sometimes if I sat really still and listened to Christian music, I felt something again.

One afternoon I'm sitting on the edge of Mom's bed and listening to my favorite song, "He's Alive," by Don Francisco. I pull my knees close to my chest and watch dust motes flicker in the sunshine streaming through Mom's window. The song is about Jesus rising from the dead and appearing to Peter. A little shiver of anticipation shoots up my spine.

I want what Mary and Peter and John had. I want to see Jesus too.

The song ends, and I get up to move the needle back on the record. I settle back on the bed, waiting. As the music swells into the final crescendo, I jump to my feet. Don sings, "He's alive and I'm forgiven, Heaven's gates are opened wide!"

My heart is racing. I know it is going to happen. I know I will see Jesus.

"Jesus, I love You!" I cry out and raise my arms to the sky. A rush of warmth fills my body, and my eyes fly open. I laugh.

At that moment, the door flies open and Mom hurries in, looking worried. "Why are you yelling in here? My goodness, this music is way, way too loud!"

I can barely contain my excitement. "Mom, Jesus is gonna appear to me! I know it!"

Mom turns down the volume and looks back at me. "What did you say?"

"I'm waiting for Jesus to appear!"

Mom is quiet, looking at me intently. In a very calm voice, she finally says, "Elizabeth, Jesus doesn't appear to people anymore. You know better than that."

"What? He doesn't?"

Mom lifts the needle from the record. "No, He doesn't."

I stare at her, confused. I can't understand why she isn't happy that I want to see Jesus. Isn't that what our family is all about?

"You're getting carried away with your emotions again. It's time you grew out of those fanciful notions."

"Yes, Mom."

After that, I stop sharing my feelings with Mom.

On the afternoon of the Rapture, I fall into a deep sleep.

I wake to silence.

For a few minutes I stare groggily at the late afternoon shadows dancing on my bedroom wall. My thumb is wet and shriveled from earnest sucking. Slowly I realize something is wrong. It is too quiet.

I sit up quickly. "Mom?"

No answer.

I dash into the hall. Nobody. Sister Nancy is gone, but the iron sits abandoned and puffing softly on the ironing board.

I run for the stairs, the sisters' bedroom flashing past me: half-folded laundry on beds, a fan oscillating slowly in an empty room. I race down the stairs, calling for Mom, Dad, Sister Nancy—anyone?

No answer.

Pausing for a moment outside the kitchen door, I try to collect my thoughts.

If the kitchen is empty, I tell myself, *then the Rapture really happened.*

The kitchen is empty.

A lone pot stands on the stove, something bubbling inside. A half-chopped carrot lies on the cutting board.

It has happened.

And I am Left Behind.

I sink to the floor and begin praying. "Dear Heavenly Father, please take me too. Please Rapture me too. Jesus, I want to meet You in the clouds with my family. I'm sorry for saying shut up. I'm sorry for complaining about eggplant casserole. I'm sorry for—"

But then I stop myself. Maybe being Left Behind is God's plan for me. Maybe I'm not supposed to ask Him to change His will for my life. I wipe my tears. And then another thought hits me: *All the worldly kids are probably freaking out right now. But I have Dad's survival plan.* My parents have trained me for this.

I stand up. It is time to check the basement stockpile.

Suddenly, the back door opens. I freeze, terrified. What if the servants of the Antichrist are already out to get me?

The kitchen door swings open, and Sister Desiree stumbles in, crying. Several other sisters cluster around her, patting her back. I stare, stunned. What is going on?

I catch sight of Mom in the hallway and yelp. I run to her, crash against her waist, and wrap my arms around her.

Mom cocks her head at me. "What's wrong?"

"The Rapture! I thought it happened! I mean, I woke up—everyone was gone!"

Mom sighs, recognizing this as yet another of my Rapture freak-outs. "The Rapture didn't happen, sweetie. Look, the only thing that happened was a tree falling in the backyard. It landed on Sister Desiree's car, poor thing."

I walk outside, squat in the driveway, and survey the wreckage. The massive pine tree that stood on the edge of our wraparound driveway has fallen over, smashing flat Sister Desiree's Pinto. Pine branches stick out of twisted metal, and shattered glass is sprayed across the driveway. I can't believe my eyes.

Dad had discussed the leaning tree as a topic of mild concern. But the tree actually falling over never seemed a real possibility. By comparison, the Rapture happening seemed far more likely. At least we'd spent way more time preparing for that kind of event.

I edge closer to the crushed car, trying to figure it out. If I stand on my tiptoes, I can see into the Pinto's flattened backseat. It is covered in broken glass and pine needles. Dirty pine sap is scattered everywhere. The scent of it fills my nose.

It just doesn't make sense. How can a stupid accident be more real than the End of the World?

All this time we've been preparing for The End. Papa George has held out a variety of options for what that might be: everyone getting Raptured or some of us being Left Behind to evangelize the rest of humanity. Or maybe the Great Tribulation and persecution of Christians would happen before the Rapture. No matter what The End looks like, Papa George is convinced it's near, and we're supposed to spend our lives preparing for it.

But now, as I survey the fallen tree, I feel something I've never felt before: doubt. Questions flood my mind.

What if there would be no Rapture, no apocalypse?

What if *everything* I believe isn't true?

Looking back, I realize these as the first independent thoughts I ever had. The day The End didn't come was the first time I wondered if that crazy lady who yelled at my dad while I preached at the street corner was right.

What if I *was* brainwashed?

PART
TWO

Chapter 9

High School Is Where the Sinners Are

D ad is sending me to public high school because I am ready to recruit my generation for the Lord. My mission: start a Bible study club so Dad can come preach to the lost souls of Sunny Hills High School.

It is a surefire evangelism strategy, Dad insists, to toss a modestly dressed, completely sheltered fourteen-year-old girl into the bowels of American culture equipped with nothing more than her huge KJV Bible. It is practically subversive to save America from godless liberals by winning their *children* for God!

The way Dad tells it, preaching the gospel to my Lost Generation will be as easy as shooting fish in a barrel. These kids are weary of their hippie parents' arbitrary morality and ready to receive the true, pure Christianity I have to offer. None of these kids knows the Bible. None of them will know how to rebut my wham-bam, take-no-prisoners style of proselytizing. My goal, Dad says, is to infiltrate their ranks, learn their weaknesses, and then sock 'em with the Good News of Jesus.

It would be a great plan if only I wasn't so terrified. On the first day of school, Mom has to practically shove me out of the car. "Be courageous for the Lord!" she crows, reaching over me and snapping the door handle open. I duck out, shaking so hard I think I might faint.

Mom locks the car door so I can't get back in and roars off with a jaunty little wave over her shoulder, her extracheerfulness the only sign she is actually worried about me. In fact, Mom isn't on board with Dad's mission for my life. She says my "sensitive and sickly constitution" won't hold up if they abandon me to The World. But Dad scoffs, dismissing this as weakness.

Hasn't he taught me to swim by throwing me into the pool? Hasn't he taught me to surf by yelling at me to paddle *toward* the waves? Hasn't he personally trained me in gospel preaching?

I watch Mom's car disappear and feel a stab of shame as tears prick my eyes. If only Dad could see me now, the sensitive and sickly crybaby, he'd remind me yet again that I was supposed to be a boy. God had even given him my name: Moses Jeremiah.

"Instead, you were a girl," Dad said, sighing. "So we named you Elizabeth Esther—at least Elizabeth gave birth to John the Baptist and Esther saved her people from destruction."

At least.

Clearly, Elizabeth Esther is a second-best savior.

I tug my baggy tunic further down over my loose leggings and scurry toward a bank of lockers. This outfit is Mom's merciful attempt to minimize some of my obvious outsider status. She's supplemented my usual wardrobe of long, flowery dresses and skirts with a few store-bought outfits—keeping them modest by buying sizes too large for me.

I press my back into a corner and settle in to observe this strange species called American Teenager swarming around me. In five minutes I see more revealing clothing and hear more cusswords than I've ever seen or heard in all my fourteen years combined. There are girls in skintight, acid-washed jeans with lattice cutouts running up their thighs. There are girls in miniskirts and teeny-tiny cheerleading outfits, and I can't imagine how they sit down without their underwear showing.

They wear huge hoop earrings and bright pink lipstick and stand in tight little circles prattling loudly about the shocking things happening in *Beverly Hills, 90210*. I have no idea who Brandon, Brenda, Dylan, and Kelly are, but it sounds as though they really need Jesus.

Next to my head, a boy slams shut a locker door and curses God in the most blasphemous way I've ever heard. I jolt out of my corner as if shocked by an electric current and run for cover, ducking my head against the lightning strike that is sure to follow.

And then I feel guilty because I am running away instead of standing up for God. I slink under the breezeway, whispering a prayer of confession, my first of many that day. "Dear Heavenly Father, please forgive me for passing an opportunity to share Jesus with that poor, sinful boy."

Suddenly, a bell shrieks through the speakers above my head. *Is there a fire? Is this an earthquake drill?* I clutch the straps of my backpack and wait for instructions. But nothing happens. I scan the crowd for an authority figure to tell me what to do.

I don't think I should move until told, so I stay frozen in place. In The Assembly, adults orchestrate a child's every move. We don't move, speak, eat, or use the restroom without first receiving permission.

But here things are different. I watch as groups of friends start breaking up and people go different directions, moving purposefully as if they know exactly what they need to do. I have my class schedule but don't know when or where I am supposed to go.

"Need help finding your first classroom?"

I look up at a tall girl, probably a senior. She is with another girl, and they are both smiling at me. I'm not sure how Dad would want me to respond to them—am I allowed to accept help from worldly kids? Dad has warned me against being suckered by nice people because even Satan appeared as an angel of light.

But I am desperate. I hold out my schedule.

"Oh, you're really close," the tall girl says. "Go down this walkway, and your English class is on the left, Mr. Wiegman's room. I had him as a freshman; he's a great teacher!"

I nod and begin walking away.

"She's so cute!" I hear the other girl say. "And she looks so scared!"

They can see I am scared? Great. Ten minutes into high school and already I am failing as a courageous evangelist to my Lost Generation.

As the weeks passed at public school, my failure as a firebrand of faith was overtaken by bigger challenges. For example, the heathens weren't throwing me to the lions. This was a problem.

How was I supposed to rescue the perishing when they kept trying to befriend me? Everywhere I turned, girls offered to hang out at lunch, coaches asked me to join the swim team, classmates invited me to their study groups, and teachers complimented my intelligence.

If only the unbelievers would start persecuting me, I thought, *maybe I could save some souls around here.*

As far as I can tell, The World isn't going to hell in a liberal handbasket. In fact, it is mostly already saved. The most popular group at Sunny Hills High School is the Christian club—a discovery I breathlessly report to Dad. "These kids are more enthusiastic than I am," I tell him. "They wear Scripture T-shirts to school and do this thing called Prayer at the Flagpole!"

Dad isn't convinced. "They probably don't study their Bibles. There are a lot of shallow Christians out there."

But Dad's assessment just doesn't match what I see in The World. I'd been prepared for persecution, blasphemy, heckling, immodesty, and rampant sinfulness. And while I do witness the worldliness of my peers, my most shocking discovery is that devout believers exist outside The Assembly. "Dad, even the Jewish girls are more devout than I am."

Dad rolls his eyes. "You don't say."

"My friend Heidi Altman just missed school for some day of atonement called Yom Kippur."

"What a good religious girl."

He doesn't mean that as a compliment. A "good Christian," a "good Jew," a "good Muslim": these are all the fake religious people Dad calls "pharisees"—those who have "a form of godliness, but denying the power thereof."

Even so, I can't figure out how I am supposed to save the lost when everybody is already found. Clearly, I am the only person who is floundering around. When I go to the school office to inquire about starting a Bible study club, I learn that only one registered Christian club can be offered at a time. Again, I report my findings to Dad.

"Well, obviously, the club we're lookin' to start is *way* different," Dad says with a sniff. "We're *studying* the Bible, not just sitting around doing happy-clappy songs and wimpy devotional readings."

"The principal doesn't see the difference."

"He wouldn't see the difference if it slapped him in the face."

The club enrollment form dangles helplessly from my fingers. I set it in front of Dad. "So, what do you want me to do? Tell the principal that our club is the *Christian* Christian club? The *real* Christian club?"

Dad snorts and pushes the form back at me. "What I want you to do is follow the calling God has on your life."

I say nothing.

For the first time in my life, I wonder whether I am following God's calling on my life or my dad's.

And there was another problem. Boys. They were everywhere.

They stared, smiled, and tried to talk with me. Josh was in my honors biology class and kept suggesting we meet in the library to study for upcoming tests. Justin was in my geometry class, and he was so hand-some I felt my heart lurch into my throat every time he smiled at me. Dietrich asked me to the movies. Adam said I was the prettiest girl in school.

I was completely blindsided. How should I respond? In The Assem-bly, we didn't believe in things like attention or flirtation or falling in love. We believed in following God's will. Feelings, pleasure, and physical at-traction were worldly and dangerous. Mom never told me I was pretty because she didn't want me to be vain. And the boys at Cornerstone Academy had made it abundantly clear that I was gross.

The only thing Dad ever told me about boys was that they all wanted One Thing. I'd learned about sex during an eighth-grade science class, but it was presented as if body parts worked like a machine: This is a penis. This is a vagina. Put them together to make a baby.

Maybe the worst thing about all the attention from boys was that it completely sabotaged my gospel-preaching mission. How to explain that I didn't go dancing because, um, that led to fornication? And that since I was saving my first kiss for my wedding day, I couldn't date either? Also, they were probably going to hell. So would they like to come to Bible study with me?

Dad said that turning boys away gave me an opportunity to see their true colors. "You'll realize what these boys are all about," he said with a knowing smile. "You go ahead and tell them no, and just you watch, they'll drop you faster than a piece of trash."

But I couldn't help it. I was fascinated. Not having brothers and being raised almost totally sequestered from boys, I found them utterly compelling. I wrote page after page in my journal about Justin, Josh, David, Dietrich, Adam, Aristotle, Erik. The attention they gave me, however fleeting, made me feel things I'd never before felt. It filled me up inside, rushing hot through my heart and mind.

After swim practice one afternoon, Justin asks me to help him reel in the lane lines and prep the pool for water-polo practice the next day. I agree and we work together, putting away paddleboards and tidying the pool deck. When we are done, everyone is gone and we are alone. I say good-bye and head into the girls' locker room.

Justin follows me.

I freeze and glance over my shoulder. "What are you doing?"

"What? Nobody's here," Justin says, shrugging. "We can be alone for a few minutes, if you want."

"I-I don't think this is a good idea," I stammer, the thrill I feel for him snapping suddenly to icy fear. "You could get in trouble. We *both* could get in trouble!"

Mom and Dad are already leery about my participation on the school swim team. I had originally signed up for swimming as sixth period PE, only to discover that the coach invited everyone to join the team. I've come to love swimming on the team and don't want anything—like getting caught with a boy in the locker room—to jeopardize that.

"We won't get in trouble if we move quick," Justin says. "Where's your locker? I'll help you carry your stuff, and my mom can give you a ride home."

Hesitantly, I lead the way to my locker and open it while Justin stands by, casually snapping his towel against his tan, muscled legs. I begin doubting myself. After all, he is a year older than I am and a starting player on the varsity water-polo team. Maybe he knows more about swim-team rules than I do. Maybe it is okay for boys to be in the girls' locker room.

I grab my towel and shoes, pull a T-shirt over my swimsuit, and stuff everything else in my swim bag. I am about to close my locker when Justin moves in and wraps his arm around my waist. His face is suddenly in mine, his lips brushing my cheek. I flinch and awkwardly lurch backward, pushing him away and banging my head against the open locker door.

"Oops!" I yell.

Something changes in Justin's face. His eyes narrow, the tender smile he's given me for weeks suddenly gone. "Silly little girl," he says, then laughs a quick, dismissive *ha-ha,* the staccato of his voice echoing off the locker-room walls.

I laugh shakily and rub the back of my head. "Ouch."

Justin turns and walks away, leaving the locker room with his swim bag slung casually over one shoulder. I follow, glancing around guiltily and hoping nobody sees us leaving together.

"Catch ya later," Justin calls over his shoulder.

I watch him trot away, not sure if I should call after him, ask if he could still give me that ride home. He never looks back.

I turn toward the strawberry fields—my shortcut home. I feel stupid and embarrassed and horribly guilty. But there is something else too: a strange elation. Maybe I am a silly little girl, but still, a cute boy has tried to kiss me. A cute boy has touched my waist and not recoiled in disgust. That is something. That is *quite* something.

A week after Justin tried to kiss me, he had his tongue down another girl's throat. I reported this to Dad—because I always reported everything to my parents—saying that the cute boy from geometry had tried to kiss me but when I said no he dropped me and moved to another girl.

"See?" Dad said. "These boys, they only want One Thing."

A month later I told Josh from biology that I wouldn't go to the dance with him. Josh started turning his back to me in class, and again, I dutifully reported this to Dad. *"Seeeee?* They're only after One Thing."

But I couldn't stop dreaming about Justin. Even when he moved on to yet a third girl, I flushed with pleasure every time I remembered the warmth of his smile. I played and replayed the scene of him trying to kiss me, except in my fantasies I didn't push him away. Like a wanton heathen I pulled him close and let him have the One Thing.

Chapter 10

God Knows If You're Wearing a Thong

B rother Bart hooks a thumb under his big rodeo belt buckle and stares around the roomful of Assembly boys and girls. He leans sideways against the podium, kicks out a cowboy boot, and crosses it over the other.

Man of God, Marlboro style.

I smooth my long skirt over my knees and wait for Brother Bart to continue lecturing on his favorite topic: modesty. It seems as though every time we have these summer youth groups, modest is hottest.

I glance around the room, a large former warehouse in an industrial building complex. A few years ago The Assembly purchased this space and converted it into a simple meeting room with plain white walls, flat blue carpet, and glaring fluorescent lighting. In the front of the room is a gigantic world map, a visual reminder of our commitment to evangelize the planet.

"Now, all you girls," Brother Bart begins in his flat midwestern voice, "y'all best listen up. If a boy can see your panty line, you're leadin' him into sexual sin."

To hear Brother Bart talk, female immodesty is responsible for practically every societal ill. Nothing seems to rile him up more than the putrefactions that are visible female curves. But the only thing I am learning from Modesty Awareness is how to have a harsh, critical view of my body—my "vile flesh," as the King James Version of the Bible calls it.

No matter how many loose-fitting skirts and baggy jeans I wear to cover my hips and butt, my body seems determined to thwart my efforts. It keeps busting out new curves. One girl I know, Mercy, has gotten so annoyed at modifying her outfits to make them modest that she's simply taken to wearing her dad's XXL shirts over baggy jeans. Better to wear a shapeless sack than risk clothing that suggests any shape whatsoever.

"Brother Bart," someone asks, "what if you just wear a thong? You know, so there aren't any visible panty lines."

From the front row Brother Bart's wife gasps.

"Wear a *what*?" he sputters, eyes bulging. "Wearin' a—wearing somethin' like that is *inherently* evil!"

A few nervous giggles erupt across the room. I chuckle too. Mostly because I am amused to hear Brother Bart use a big word like "inherently." Two-syllable words are more his thing. Then again, we all know about inherent evil: our desperately wicked hearts, television shows like *Beverly Hills, 90210*, processed foods, the Devil's Music (a.k.a. anything with a syncopated beat), dancing, drinking, and now, skimpy underwear.

The questioner persists. "But what if nobody *knows* you're wearing a thong?"

I swivel in my seat, looking for the girl asking these daring questions. It is Jael. No surprise here. From an Assembly in the Midwest, Jael is known for her semipermanent state of Struggling in Her Walk with the Lord. Of course—much to Brother Bart's dismay—Jael and I have become quick friends, bound by our mutual love of sarcasm and talking about boys.

Brother Bart has pulled me aside more than once to warn me against pursuing friendship with Jael because she "has issues with authority." But

I know why Jael struggles: even as a teenager she still gets spankings. I think her lot is unlucky but not outrageous—my own parents only just stopped spanking me a year earlier, when I turned thirteen. This is just how things are.

Brother Bart grips the podium and glares at Jael. Unaccustomed to being challenged, Brother Bart seems unable to process what is happening. He huffs into the microphone a few times before his wife, Sister Jo-May, comes to his rescue.

"Lover," she says, half rising from her chair, "if I may?"

"Yes, lover. Please do," says Brother Bart. They always refer to each other as "lover," the fundamentalist version of a public display of affection.

"Well, my goodness," Sister Jo-May declares, pulling the microphone down to her level. "It's not as if *nobody* knows you're wearing immodest undergarments. After all"—she leans in closer, deadly serious—"God knows if you're wearing a thong!"

When the room bursts into laughter, Sister Jo-May looks stunned. She is one of those women whose intentional piety is accidentally funny. Brother Bart flicks the microphone away from her, a dismissive gesture that makes her turn toward us and sternly shake her head *no, no, stop laughing.*

Brother Bart pounds the podium. "That's enough!" he booms. "That weren't a joke!"

But we can't stop laughing. Hearing Sister Jo-May say the word *thong* is like hearing an Amish woman say "fuck."

"Tell you what!" Brother Bart roars. "Y'all don't stop laughing at my wife, I'm gonna cancel me our beach trip!"

That brings us up short. We are desperate for fun.

"Have I ever told y'all the story of dog-poop brownies?" Brother Bart asks, cranking the microphone back to his height. Nobody says a word. Brother Bart is fond of asking rhetorical questions.

"Well, when I was a little kid, my mom had a habit of makin' big, beautiful plates of brownies. One day she told me to go ahead and help myself. I was about to pop that brownie in my mouth when she added, all casual-like, 'Don't worry, I only put a little dog poop in 'em.'"

Brother Bart laughs and Sister Jo-May joins in, the two of them nodding at each other as if this is the most hilarious story ever. Across the room, a few youth group counselors chuckle halfheartedly, a show of support more than anything else.

"Do you think I ate that brownie?" Brother Bart asks.

Nobody answers.

"My guess is noooo!" singsongs Sister Jo-May again, always the helpful helpmeet.

I glance at Jael and she rolls her eyes. I smile into my lap.

Brother Bart is talking again. "You're right, lover! I didn't eat that brownie because all it takes is a little poop to ruin the whole thing."

"Aaa-*men* to that!" Sister Jo-May says, raising her hand in an I-can-testify gesture.

"Can anyone guess why I'm telling this story?" Brother Bart asks. "Y'all know it's not a *real* story, right? It's what we call a…a…" He pauses, searching for the right description.

"A morality tale?" his wife offers.

"Amen! Praise the Lord, the morality here is that dog-poop brownies is like sexual sin. Just a pinch a sexual defilement ruins the whole person."

Brother Bart grins at us, clearly pleased with his powers of comparative analysis. I feel my stomach clench. *Here we go again.* Brother Bart is revving up the rhetoric, tapping the podium now with barely restrained excitement. I brace myself for impact.

"You get you a girl sportin' immodest undergarments, and there's no tellin' what other sorta defiling business she into!" Brother Bart declares. "Young ladies, y'all listen up! If you wanna attract a godly man for a husband, ain't gonna happen if you showing off your body to the whole world. No good man wants a woman who dresses like a prostitute, am I right, lover?"

Brother Bart glances at Sister Jo-May, and she nods with glowing approval. If the way they dress their daughters is any indication, "dressing like a prostitute" means anything more revealing than Victorian blouses and long skirts.

"You got somethin' you wanna add to this?" Brother Bart asks his wife.

Sister Jo-May fairly leaps out of her chair. She folds her hands on the podium and trades her pious voice for a chiding one. "Young ladies, let's check our hearts, okay? This isn't just about underwear now, is it? This is about the motives of our hearts before God. Being modest is about how we walk, how we sit, how we bend over, whether we're drawing attention to ourselves through flirtatious behavior or tone of voice. I mean, ladies, have you considered that wearing your purse across your chest can be very distracting for a man? And how can we call ourselves Christians if we're wearing—" Sister Jo-May glances at her husband. "What was it we were discussing yesterday?"

Brother Bart gestures at his chest, pointing from nipple to nipple. Sister Jo-May's face lights up. "That's right!" she crows. "Bras, them new-fangled ones." She turns back to the room and scans our faces slowly. Brother Bart stands behind her, glaring at the room to keep us from laughing.

"How—*how* can you call yourself a Christian," pleads Sister Jo-May, "if you're wearing a push-up bra?"

And impact. The boys in the room guffaw, elbowing each other. I want to crawl under my chair. Sister Jo-May gives us all a withering stare.

These modesty discussions always derail somehow, becoming a train wreck of awkwardness. I stare at my notebook, biting my lip hard.

I wear a padded bra, but not because I am trying to be sexy. I wear it because Dad so often comments about the outrage of being able to see a woman's nipples through her shirt that I am terrified he might see mine. Padded bras are the only way to make sure that doesn't happen.

Sister Jo-May isn't done. "Sisters in Christ, I ask you, I plead with you by the blood of the Lamb!" She seems suddenly on the verge of tears. "Do you really want to have to tell your future husband about all the men you've led into sexual sin? Do you really want to stand before God and answer for tempting your brothers in Christ?"

"God forbid!" answers Brother Bart.

Sister Jo-May is almost shrieking now, as if higher decibels can cover up her urge to cry. "Young women! Would you truly defile yourself with the passing pleasures of this world rather than present yourself a spotless bride on your wedding day? Young men, do you truly want a woman who has given herself away to other men—even if only through lust?"

She pauses and draws a deep, ragged breath. Brother Bart puts a hand on her shoulder, signaling it is time to stop, and she bows her head submissively, backing away from the podium.

"I always a-ppreciate a godly woman's perspective, amen? Thank you for that, lover." Brother Bart looks around the room. "I hope y'all are listening. Let's ask God to help us recommit to purity. We're gonna take out our notebooks and write three things we're gonna do to keep our purity. Please turn those lists in to your counselors when you're done so they can keep you accountable."

I turn to a blank page in my notebook. And then I sit there, staring at it. *Why are we doing this? What is the point? How many times are we sup-posed to "recommit" ourselves to saving our first kiss—not to mention our first sexual encounter—for our future spouse? Does God want me to burn my padded bra?*

As I chew the top of my pencil, I suddenly remember a play I read in school the previous year: Henrik Ibsen's *A Doll's House*. The play had angered and excited me. I was angry about the portrayal of family life as stultifying and oppressive. But I couldn't deny certain similarities. It struck me as terribly depressing that here in 1992 the rights of women in The Assembly were no more advanced for us than for Nora in Ibsen's 1879 play. The modesty rules, the purity commitments, the roles re-quired of us because we were female—there was no end to the controls men placed on our lives.

"Elizabeth, have you finished your list?"

It is my counselor, Vivian—a single twenty-something, who is living in my training home and volunteering her time to help with us teens.

I shake my head. "Sorry, I was thinking." I know I am having rebel-lious thoughts again. If I voice them, I'll get in trouble. I can't let anyone know that the books and plays I am reading in school are opening my mind to new and different ideas. *The Stranger* by Albert Camus rattled my worldview. And then *1984* by George Orwell. When Dad saw me reading that, he commented that the United States government was like Big Brother. I didn't dare tell him what I was thinking—that Big Brother was actually The Assembly.

Vivian pats my shoulder and whispers in my ear. "Write a vague purity commitment. I have to turn this in to Brother Bart."

"Thanks for the tip," I whisper back. "Maybe *you* should commit to not running around the house naked."

Vivian snorts, attracting a stern look from Brother Bart. "You know

I only do that when nobody's home," she whispers. "Don't tell your parents!"

I grin at Vivian. Of all the women who have lived in our communal home over the years, Vivian is one of my favorites. Her bright, bubbly personality is a welcome relief from the drudgery of endless meetings and rules. Vivian has befriended me, talking to me as if I am a real person with important feelings and thoughts. She never treats me as though I am Papa George's granddaughter or some kind of outreach opportunity.

But even Vivian's natural optimism and contagious spontaneity can't overcome The Assembly oppression. She's recently confessed to "struggling" and reminded me that it is more important to marry according to God's will than to marry for love. I don't know what is going on with her, but I am worried. (My fears would be realized a few weeks later when Vivian ran away with a guy from work and got married in Las Vegas.)

But at our youth group meeting, all I can think about is finishing my list. I hurriedly scribble in my notebook: *1. Guard my heart. 2. Bring my thoughts under the control of Christ.* I tear the paper out and hand it to Vivian.

Brother Bart returns to the podium to lead us in a closing prayer. He asks us to confess silently in our hearts our impure thoughts and recommit to purity.

I bow my head and confess the one terrible sin I am guilty of committing at least three times a week. It is the sin I believe nobody else commits—especially not other girls. I know it is evidence of my particularly wicked, sexually impure heart. And if Brother Bart is right, this one sin ruins everything.

I clutch my hands in my lap, dig my fingernails into my knuckles, and ask Jesus to forgive me for locking myself in the bathroom and touching myself. Sometimes even on Sundays.

Chapter 11

An Escape Plan

Ye cannot serve God and mammon. This we knew. But by the end of my sophomore year, I was wondering if maybe God made exceptions. For instance, could I serve God and university?

I tried not to entertain rebellious thoughts, but a contrarian seed was growing in my mind. One of my teachers had pulled me aside and told me I showed promise as a writer. Would I consider applying for a spot on the school newspaper? And a guidance counselor told me I had a fair shot at a private university if I continued to pull in excellent grades.

A private university! It was a whisper of hope, a chance at having a future away from my family and The Assembly. Until my teachers suggested it, I'd never considered that an Assembly-free future could be unlocked by my intellect. It was an intoxicating possibility.

The question was whether I could live both lives: doing enough to please Dad as the good Assembly girl so as not to arouse his suspicions while also creating a secret escape plan for myself. It was risky. It was downright rebellious.

Escape was my only hope, even if it meant abandoning my calling to recruit my Lost Generation for the Lord.

Mom and Dad were suspicious. They kept summoning me to "little chats" where they peppered me with questions, scrutinized my homework assignments and swim schedule, went through my backpack, and had me try on various outfits to make sure they were modest. They wanted to know why I was so busy, why I wasn't talking with them, if I was reading my Bible every day. They suspected I was hiding something.

And I was. I was making plans to leave for college.

I'd already competed for—and earned—a coveted writing position on the high school newspaper, won Most Improved Swimmer during my freshman year, set a school record in the fifty-yard butterfly, and was pulling in good grades in my honors classes. My guidance counselors told me these things would make for a great college application, and my desperate hope was that I'd earn a scholarship at a university far from home, far from The Assembly.

But my parents had noticed how preoccupied I was, and they were not pleased.

One afternoon when I am sixteen, they call me into their bedroom for yet another "little chat." This time, I am really worried. The Head Steward—our communal home's house manager—has tattled to Mom about my failure to complete my daily and weekly chores. The Head Steward has given me fifteen minutes of extra work for each incomplete chore, but since I so often delay "doing my time," I've racked up over thirty hours.

I enter Mom and Dad's bedroom trying to smile cheerfully. My hands are shaking, so I place them solidly on my hips.

"Sit down," Dad commands from his seat at the bedroom desk. He has a notebook and Bible in front of him—ready for battle.

"The Head Steward tells me you've neglected to scrub the grout in all the showers," Mom says, tapping a notebook she holds in her lap. She is perched in her favorite armchair with all her training-home binders, folders, menus, and a few home décor catalogs propped beside her. She looks up, lowers her reading glasses, and stares at me over the rims. "Do you have an explanation for this irresponsible behavior?"

"Well, I—"

"What we want to know," Dad interjects, "is why you're piling up so much consequence time and why you think it's okay not to work it off before the new week begins. Elizabeth, failing to do your duty doesn't just inconvenience others; it's a failure in your duty to God."

In my parents' view, everything in life is spiritual. My incomplete chores aren't so much about dirty tile grout as they are about the state of my (dirty) soul.

I sit on the edge of their bed and tell myself to remain calm. I fold my hands in my lap and take a deep breath. "Well, I've gotten behind on my consequence time because I've been busy with school," I say. "I'm taking the pre-SAT soon."

Dad yanks an ankle up over his knee and leans back in his chair, examining me intently. "What's this about some school newspaper job Mom tells me you got? Won't that interfere with your responsibilities here at home?"

"It shouldn't be that bad," I answer. "I'll stay after school one day a week to help lay out the paper, type up articles and stuff."

Dad frowns. "Hmm. Mom tells me that while I was gone on my preaching journey, you missed a bunch of weekly meetings."

I feel a quick jolt of heat and glance at Mom. She is flipping through her chore charts, seemingly unruffled by Dad's line of questioning. When Dad is gone—sometimes for three months at a time—she is the one who encourages me to work hard in school and says it is fine to skip Assembly meetings for homework.

"I…I'm not missing meetings because I'm backsliding or something," I say. "I'm taking all these honors classes and swimming competitively—Hey, Dad! Did you know I qualified for prelims at state finals this year?"

"Huh." He isn't smiling. "Sounds to me like your schedule is full."

What is this leading up to? "I'll work off my consequence time this weekend, I promise!"

"She really *is* working hard," Mom mutters, scribbling something in her notebook without looking up.

"She may be working hard," Dad answers. "But does she have the right priorities? *That* is the question." He flips through his Bible, searching for a verse.

I watch him look for a passage that will prove his point and wonder why Mom isn't defending me. I look at her again, trying to read her facial expression. Mom catches my eye and smiles benignly, her face a mask of serenity. But she looks away quickly, and I see the hint of something else in her eyes—sadness, maybe?

I suddenly realize that since Dad got home from his preaching trip last week, Mom hasn't seen her friends at all. When Dad was gone, Mom was relaxed and happy. She went out to dinner and played racquetball with single women in The Assembly. She let me stay home from meetings and even allowed me to hang out with my own friends occasionally.

But when Dad got home, life got strict again. Dad usually spends the first week home recovering from jet lag. But the second week he goes on the warpath, calling family meetings and ordering everyone around because it is time to "put my own house back in order!" Dad never approves of Mom spending time away from home, and I suddenly wonder if this "little chat" is Dad's way of punishing not only me but her.

Dad finds the chapter he is looking for and runs his finger down the page. "Ah! There it is!" he says. "Now, listen to this, Elizabeth. First Samuel 2:30 says, 'Them that honour me I will honour, and they that despise me shall be lightly esteemed.'" Dad looks up, raising his eyebrows at me expectantly.

I know what is required. He wants me to explain how this verse applies to my life. "Um. If we honor the Lord, He honors us?" I offer.

"That's right, and for our family that means we attend all the weekly meetings, all the Sunday meetings, and the outreaches. You're setting a bad example. You are not honoring the Lord with your time."

Against my will, my eyes fill with tears. "That's not true!"

"I'm sure you're working hard," Dad says. "But you're not prioritizing the things of the Lord."

"Mom, don't you want me to earn good grades?" I ask.

She beams one of her extralarge smiles at me. "Of course, sweetheart. But what your father is saying is that we've noticed you're not fulfilling your responsibilities here at home. You're overcommitted to things outside the Lord's will."

"You mean, I'm overcommitted to things outside *The Assembly*," I say.

Dad stands and steps toward me. "Watch it, Elizabeth."

I can feel myself hurtling toward a cliff. Even though I desperately want to leave home for college, I just as desperately want his blessing. It is a weird conundrum. By now I know something is terribly wrong in The Assembly, and I want out. But I also love my parents. We don't show much natural affection between us (all the spanking and rigid "Christian lifestyle" have preempted that), but I still don't want to dishonor them.

I want Dad's approval, if only so I can escape to college without provoking his wrath. I'd started a Bible study at school so he could see how serious I was about being a Good Christian. Every Wednesday at lunch we met in my history teacher's classroom to read our Bibles and share from prepared chapter summaries. When Dad wasn't traveling, his dynamic preaching packed the Bible club with kids sitting on the floor or standing against the walls. Dad came alive when he had an audience and thrived on the attention of young people flocking to him for spiritual counsel.

But now, faced with Dad's disapproval of my schedule, I realize that even the success of the Bible club isn't enough to earn his blessing on my college plans. His interests begin and end with The Assembly. Dad says he is concerned with Issues of Eternal Significance—like growing and expanding The Assembly—so he doesn't have time to come to my swim meets or awards ceremonies.

So far, I've worked his disinterest to my advantage: if he doesn't care about what is important to me, he certainly won't find out about my escape plan. I would reveal it to them *after* I was accepted to a college far away. That would force their hand. They'd be so proud of my academic achievements and my commitment to being a Good Christian that they'd send me off without disowning me.

For years, I've poured my heart out in my journal, dreaming of the new life I wanted to live:

March 25, 1993. If I could have anything, I'd want freedom. All of my life I've been told what to do, who to become, how to become it—and now, I want to become it on my own. College, life, love—is all just around the corner, a whole other world waits for me. I know I'm terribly selfish but these yearnings, these glimmerings of hope, these blossoming dreams will never become true. I want to get AWAY! But how? Have I the money? Have I the support? No. If I work hard, pray hard, and live hard, God helping me, I can do it. Oh, how I want it. For now, I must be content with breaking the rules silently [and] the triumphant feeling I get.

But now I wonder if my plan is simply a foolish fantasy. I take a deep breath and wipe my tears.

"Listen, Wiz," Dad says in a more conciliatory tone, "your mother and I only want God's best for you. Don't you believe that?"

I suck in some air. "Sure."

"So!" he proclaims—as if this were the best news ever—"*of course* we'll support any plans of yours that are in line with God's will for you!"

I wait, knowing he isn't finished.

"And how does God reveal His will for Elizabeth?" Dad roars, opening his arms to an imaginary crowd. He turns toward me and, as if this were a game show, points a pretend microphone at me.

I pause, refusing to play along. "Umm..."

Dad guffaws and slaps his knee. "Come on, Wiz! Don't spoil the fun. You know the answer—it's an easy question! How does God reveal His will for you?"

"I don't think I know."

"Well, since I'm your father and have authority over you until you're married...God's will for you comes through me!"

From her armchair, Mom chuckles. She is endlessly amused by Dad's antics. Or at least she pretends to be.

I feel my armpits prick with sweat, a sure sign I am getting stressed out. But remaining calm and unflustered is my only chance for keeping my escape plan safe, secret, and intact. I take another deep breath and wipe my palms on my skirt. "Dad, what are you telling me?"

Dad grins. "You're a smart one, Wiz."

I wait.

"Your father just complimented you," Mom says. She always refers to him as "your father" when we are having a serious discussion.

"Oh, sorry. Thank you, Dad."

"That's my girl!" Dad whoops. "I knew you'd come around! Now just keep that good attitude because by giving up your position on the school newspaper you're honoring the Lord."

It takes me a moment to register what Dad is saying. When I begin talking, my voice has gone all squeaky. "Did you just say I have to resign my newspaper position?"

Dad slaps my shoulder playfully. "Did I stutter? Or actually, does God stutter?"

Mom chuckles again, wagging her head at silly ol' Daddy.

I feel my throat tightening. Earning a spot on the school newspaper was a huge achievement. I love writing, and for the first time in my life, I have somewhere to write and a journalism teacher who believes in me. Working for the paper is also a vital piece of my escape plan—without it, private universities won't even look at my college application.

I swallow hard and decide to speak my mind. What do I have to lose? "Dad, I want to move away for college. I really think I have a shot at earning a scholarship, but I need this newspaper job to do it. I don't want to disobey you. I want to go to college with your blessing."

Dad looks genuinely shocked. "Move away? How could that possibly be God's will for you? You'd be forsaking The Assembly!"

I look at my mother. "Mom, please," I whisper.

She looks up from her catalog, her face smooth and unflustered with just a hint of mild annoyance at my distress. This is the face she puts on when Dad is home—the mask of a compliant, submissive wife.

"Elizabeth, your father is right," she trills in a breezy, smiley voice. "I've been wondering how to pull you back from 'the way that leadeth unto destruction.' Surely you don't believe it's God's will for you to move away from your father's protection and covering!"

I am falling off the cliff, the edges of my vision blurring. My neck is scorching hot, and I want to scream. Instead, I leap to my feet. "Anything else?" I squawk, my voice breaking.

Dad chortles and darts at me. "I see a bee come out the barn, sayin' I'll do you no harm!" It is a tickle game. He pokes his finger hard into my armpit. "Bzzzzzzzz!"

I spin away from him. "No!" It is the most honest thing I've ever said to him. *No* is a word I'm not allowed to say to my father. I know I'll pay for it.

Dad catches my arm and squeezes it so tightly I gasp in pain. "Can't you let ol' Dad have some fun?" he says. And then in a mock baby voice: "Why da bad addy-tude, Wiz-a-wif?" Still chuckling, as if this is all a fun game, he clamps his arms around me and crushes me against his chest. I resist and he squeezes harder, smashing my face until I can't breathe.

Panic. *Panic.*

I am a little girl again, trapped between Dad's legs while he tickles me mercilessly. If I scream or cry or try to break free, he tickles me harder and holds me tighter.

"I won't let you go until you totally surrender!" he'd laugh.

"Daddy, please!" I'd cry.

"What's worse than a tornado?" he'd yell.

"Please *don't*!"

"A titty twister!" And then he'd grab my little-girl nipples and twist them until I screamed.

Now, through the blur of my fear, I hear Mom. "I think we can let Elizabeth calm down in her room."

I push away from Dad.

Mom intervenes. "Let her *go*." She sometimes does this when she thinks Dad's games have gone too far.

Dad releases me, and I burst into sobs, sucking in ragged breaths. "Oh, stop being a crybaby," Dad says. "I was just teasin' ya."

I gulp, willing myself to stop crying. If I argue further, I know they'll start taking away my other "privileges": talking on the phone, swimming on the school team, driving, doing volunteer work. If I get too rebellious, they might pull me out of high school altogether. At least if I obey for now, maybe I can still attend a local college.

I drag my sleeve over my face and try to smile at Dad, demonstrating my total surrender.

"Well, then," he says, "how about a big hug and kiss from my girl?"

I don't want to hug or kiss. I don't want to touch him. But if I refuse, they might punish me more. I don't want to find out what that might be.

I hug Dad. I hug Mom.

"The dinner bell is about to ring," Mom says, patting my back. "Go freshen your face and brush your hair."

Chapter 12

Cult Girl in Love

There's a kiss, and then there's A Kiss.

My first boyfriend was a secret. I tucked the secret of him into myself like an insurance policy against the impossibility of escaping The Assembly. Ever since Dad forbade me to leave home for college, I'd kinda given up on school. I did just enough to maintain a B-plus average. I quit the extracurricular activities that were going to help round out my college application. I even considered quitting the swim team. Instead of academics, I focused all my attention on boys.

Boys became my reason for living.

Aristotle was unlike any boy I'd ever met. He was gentle and kind, soft-spoken and deferential. He came from a hardworking Filipino family and had recently transferred to my public high school from a private Catholic one. We traded casual banter during swim practice, and I kept track of all his assists and goals during water-polo games. We had an honors class together, and he was in my study group.

The first time he said he liked me was while we painted a house for a school-sponsored charity event. I said I liked him too but admitted my parents strictly prohibited dating. He said this was fine since his parents didn't want him dating a white girl.

One day, Aristotle asks if he can walk me home. Swim practice has ended, and the late afternoon sunlight slanting across the strawberry fields behind our school is irresistibly golden. I say yes.

Aristotle's face breaks into a huge grin, his deep brown eyes holding mine for a long moment. I look away, a hot flush of excitement rising in my cheeks. I love the way he looks at me—as if I am the most precious and desirable girl he's ever known.

We walk slowly, edging through a gap in the chain-link fence that surrounds the strawberry fields behind Sunny Hills High School. Although the fields are technically off-limits, students use them as a walking shortcut. During school hours, the fields are full of migrant farm workers. But now, in the late afternoon, everything is quiet.

We follow a path worn between the rows, and as we trot down a small hill, Aristotle reaches for my hand, steadying me. We reach the bottom of the hill, and he doesn't let go. I don't pull away. A line of eucalyptus trees shelter us from view. For a moment, we have complete privacy.

Aristotle turns to me. "I have something for you," he says and pulls an envelope from his backpack. "Don't open it now. Just read it when you get home."

I feel awkward and try to pretend I don't care. "Oooh, a mushy-gushy love letter?"

He looks stricken, glancing away in embarrassment.

I feel lame. He is showing me his heart, and I am cracking jokes. The truth is, I want love letters, words of endearment, affection, and devotion.

"I'm sorry!" I cry and spontaneously throw my arms around his neck. Aristotle startles a bit, but he recovers quickly and wraps his arms around me. We stand still together.

After a few moments like that, he whispers into my neck, "May I kiss you?"

I nod against his shoulder. I know this won't be like my first, disappointing kiss—that awkward, back-of-the-gym mash up at a school dance I'd snuck out to last year. This kind of kiss is different. This is my first *real* kiss, the kind that means something.

His lips meet mine, and they are soft, warm, and gentle. He takes his time. We kiss and kiss. I feel as if I am being chosen.

I am suddenly very present, exquisitely aware of every tiny detail. I've only felt such heightened awareness when scared. This is the exact opposite. My stomach muscles relax, my breathing slows, every inch of my body responds to his warm embrace.

Slowly, everything bad drifts far, far away. All my feelings of not being good enough, of never having enough love, dissipate in the glow of his affection. I want to stay right here in this moment forever.

When we finally break apart, the sun is almost gone. It is dusk. I have to run if I am going to get home before dinner.

We kiss once more, and then I am running across the field. I am as light as air. I can run a million miles. I can fly. I don't care whether I get punished. This feeling. This *feeling*!

Mom is driving through the neighborhood next to the strawberry fields when I come flying around the corner. She pulls over looking equal parts relieved and angry.

"Where were you? I've been driving around for the past twenty minutes! You were supposed to be home an hour ago!"

I climb into the car. "I'm sorry; swim practice went late."

I am lying. Intentionally. A twinge of guilt breaks through my giddiness, but I ignore it. This euphoric feeling—it is everything.

Mom drives me home, and I turn my head to the window so she

can't see me smiling. Inside, something has shifted on its axis. I want more of that bliss.

One kiss and I am hooked.

The euphoria lasted for three months.

It was all a secret. We never made it official, even though our closest school friends gave us knowing winks. We communicated through hand-written notes passed to each other in the hall. He met me after swim practice and walked me home through the strawberry fields. We kissed beneath trees. He whispered French poetry in my ear. The secrecy heightened the intensity.

I had never felt this *good* in all my life.

I felt alive.

I kept waking up at night. I was having unwelcome, unpleasant thoughts.

For example, it occurred to me that plunging myself into relationships with boys did not fix my real problem—mainly, The Assembly. Falling in love didn't make me less angry about being forced to resign the newspaper job. Having a boyfriend was a poor consolation prize for being stripped of my dream of going away to college.

And I had made another mistake: believing romantic intensity was intimacy. But even while secretly making out in strawberry fields and waking up scared in the middle of the night, I sensed the high would wear off eventually. If I could feel that high, what would it feel like to come crashing down?

"Elizabeth, you're hiding something from me."

Dad's voice sends a jolt of fear racing up my spine. For almost three months I've successfully hidden my relationship with Aristotle. But the previous night, Dad and Mom had unexpectedly shown up at the movie theater where I was on a secret double date. My parents had given me permission to see the C. S. Lewis movie *Shadowlands,* but only because I said I was going with a girlfriend.

"Look at me," says Dad.

I look up at him, shivering slightly in the chilly December air. He insists we take a walk together—away from the house, away from listening ears. I know I am in trouble.

"I don't want you to ever see that boy again, do you understand? You are not to go anywhere with him, talk on the phone with him, or hang out with him at school."

I nod, trying to keep a calm face. But tears are forming in my eyes.

"Your mother and I have decided to ground you for a month. You've broken our trust. I'm not about to let the world steal my daughter. Satan wants to sift you like wheat, Elizabeth."

I dash at messy tears running down my cheeks.

Dad hands me the cowboy bandanna he always keeps in his pocket. It is gross, but I don't care. I know worse things are coming—like having to break up with Aristotle. I honk noisily into the fabric.

Dad steers me to a nearby park bench, and we sit down. "Now, do you really want to bring shame to our family by pursuing a life of lies and self-centeredness? That's the road you're going down, Elizabeth. These plans you have might seem good, but the Bible says, 'The way of a fool is right in his own eyes: but he that hearkeneth unto counsel is wise.'"

"I know what the Bible says," I snap.

"Ah, out of the heart the mouth speaks."

I turn away from him, clenching my hands. I cross my arms and pinch the insides until I gasp in pain. I'd discovered the secret trick of using physical pain to distract myself from emotional pain. The huge rush of adrenaline I experienced after hurting myself blotted out my mental and emotional desperation. It made me feel okay again.

"Elizabeth, your behavior is jeopardizing everything God has for you," Dad says, pulling my shoulder to turn me back toward him. "Do you really want to miss out on God's eternal plan for your life?"

I say nothing, just stare at the gray hills surrounding our neighborhood park. The winter rains have yet to turn the hills green—it is a tiny seasonal change I wait for all year. I tune out Dad's voice and concentrate on the leaves scattered on the cement, the feeling of my toes growing cold inside my sneakers.

I am tired. I am only seventeen, and yet I am so very tired.

Maybe Dad is right. Maybe God really does want me to stay in The Assembly. After all, I am sick of getting in trouble, being grounded, lying to cover up my double life, putting on the Good Pastor's Kid show. I feel guilty about all the times I've kissed Aristotle. If Dad knew how much kissing I've done, he'd say my purity is lost. What if he is right? What if I am defiled?

"Are you ready to repent, Elizabeth?" Dad asks.

I bow my head and surrender. Dad places a hand on my shoulder, and I confess my sins.

We walk home in the failing December light, Dad whistling the tune to his favorite hymn, "Rock of Ages." When we are almost home, he urges me to sing along with him.

> *Rock of Ages, cleft for me,*
> *Let me hide myself in thee;*
> *Let the water and the blood,*
> *From thy riv'n side which flowed,*
> *Be of sin the double cure,*
> *Cleanse me from its guilt and power.*

I am in the emergency room, and Dad is standing at the foot of my bed talking in hushed tones with Mom. All I remember is breaking out in a cold sweat, starting to shake all over, and then nothing.

It's been two weeks since I broke up with Aristotle. I never knew heartbreak could feel like physical sickness. I've lost my appetite, lost weight, lost the will to go to school, succumbed to a bad case of bronchitis.

Mom and Dad are arguing with the doctors, insisting I'm having a reaction to the antibiotics. But the doctors disagree, saying my symptoms are more consistent with a panic attack. "Is Elizabeth under a lot of emotional strain? Has this kind of thing happened to her in the past?"

I roll over onto my side and wish the bronchitis would get worse so I'd have to stay in the hospital. I don't want to go home. I don't want to go back to my life.

I close my eyes, trying to ignore the sound of Dad informing the doctors that nobody in his family struggles with fake illnesses like anxiety because we have faith in the Lord! "Are you a believer, Doctor?"

"Hey," says a voice. I open my eyes. Next to my bed a nurse is crouched at eye level. He takes my hand. "You're gonna be okay. You're alive and it's a beautiful night out there. You can see the stars."

I nod mutely.

"Let's get this IV outta your arm, all right?"

The doctors leave and Dad is huffy. My "fake illness" has made him late for prayer meeting. He decides to let Mom handle everything, saying the brethren need him. I keep my face turned away and ignore him when he says he'll pray for me.

"Try not to take it personally," Mom says, once Dad is gone. She sits on the bed and pats my legs reassuringly. "Dad loves you very much, but sometimes the only way he knows how to show it is by going into preacher mode. Can you try to understand your father?"

Oh, yes. I understand my father. I don't even have to try.

Breaking up with Aristotle didn't break my craving for love. My new plan was to attract the right Assembly boy, hook myself onto his dreams, and let him carry me away.

So I went straight from Aristotle to Nathaniel. Nathaniel, I thought, would be different. His parents ran The Assembly in Chicago, and Papa George spoke highly of him. He winked at me and said, "Nathaniel would make an excellent choice." This was what every good Assembly girl dreamed of: a young marriage followed immediately by a slew of babies.

Nathaniel was smart, athletic, and family approved. Also, marrying him would take me far away from home. Clearly, this was God's choice for me.

At first, my strategy appeared to be working. Nathaniel and I wrote letters for a whole year—well, actually I wrote long, descriptive epistles, and he scribbled short, jokey notes.

I sent him my poetry, and he sent me a pair of his beat-up wrestling shoes. I mailed him a lock of my hair, and he mailed me a picture of his sister's pet rabbit. I tried to build an emotional connection by using beautiful stationery and carefully signing and dating my letters. He'd reply on a torn piece of notebook paper, dating the year as 2076. To my fraught descriptions of life in The Assembly, Nathaniel's signature reply was: "You'll be fine."

Still, when Mom and Dad saw the letters arriving from Chicago, they smiled and advised me to pray about whether Nathaniel was my future husband. It was hard to imagine marrying a seventeen-year-old guy whose idea of a love letter was a story about his brother barfing sloppy joes. The more I prayed about Nathaniel, the more convinced I became that he was The One.

By the time Nathaniel advanced to signing his letters with "Love you so much," Papa George offered to pay for a flight to Chicago so I could meet Nathaniel's family. But since dating was forbidden, I was told not to talk about the reason for my trip. In The Assembly, we believed in courtship—which was just a fancy way of saying church leadership approved and arranged marriages.

Basically, Papa George was encouraging my potential courtship with Nathaniel while also telling me to pretend I was visiting Chicago to see a girlfriend, Jael. This duplicitous awkwardness should have been my first hint of impending doom, but as a pastor's kid, I was accustomed to pretending to make my family look good. And this time, I had a vested interest: I *really* wanted to see my future husband.

I take great care packing my bags for the trip. I choose my most beautiful dresses and sweaters, making sure to pack extra long slips for full modesty coverage. In a Ziploc bag, I wrap my favorite necklace and my one pair of clip-on earrings—Assembly girls don't have body piercings. The night before I depart, I paint my toes and fingernails a natural shade of pink and curl my hair in a cascade of ringlets.

I am so excited and nervous I can hardly sleep. *Will Nathaniel's family like me? Will Nathaniel declare his intentions?* If Nathaniel tells me he loves me, I know I will happily betroth myself to him and wait until Papa George gives us his permission to wed. I figure I'll be married a year after high school graduation.

When I arrive in Chicago, I stay with Jael's family, but Nathaniel's parents take me to lunch at a fancy deli on Michigan Avenue and have me over for dinner. One day they invite me to go skiing with them. Nathaniel seems happy to see me, but he also seems, well, like Nathaniel, barf jokes and all.

I keep telling myself to focus on the tiny signs of his affection, whispering, "Love you so much, love you so much" to myself, as if the way he signs his letters is the promise of our married future.

The day of our ski trip arrives, and Nathaniel's parents pick me up while it is still dark. I bundle into the back of their minivan with Nathaniel and his three siblings.

Despite the early hour, Nathaniel's mom is chirpy and cheerful as ever, inquiring whether I'd prefer listening to Keith Green or a cappella hymns. I choose Keith Green, and we all settle in for a long drive out to the hilly countryside.

I am tucked into the bench seat behind Nathaniel, a great big blanket over my body. I wonder how we will talk since he is facing away from me. If I am going to build an emotional bond, I *need* conversation. I need something more than jokey notes.

Suddenly I feel something fumbling under my blanket. I lean forward and realize it is Nathaniel's hand, reaching back to touch me.

My heart freezes. This is definitely forbidden. I feel a moment of panic: Nathaniel is supposed to be different. He knows the rules. He knows we aren't supposed to touch until after we are betrothed. I'm not in rebellion anymore. I want my relationship with Nathaniel to be done The Assembly Way. No hiding, no secrets, all family approved. In The Assembly, it isn't just about remaining an intact virgin; it is about being completely pure—no kissing, no hand holding, no hugging, no touching of any kind.

By Assembly standards, I am already defiled because of what I've done with Aristotle. I so long for a do-over, a fresh start with Nathaniel. I want to be the spotless bride, proudly presented to my husband by my adoring father.

But it is too late. Nathaniel's hand finds my foot, and he lifts it up, tucking it in next to his body. I hold my breath, waiting for something worse. But that is it. He simply holds my foot and gently rubs my ankle through my jeans.

Slowly, I relax. The warmth of his hand is magic, intoxicating. I begin to feel the old, familiar rush. I want more. I lean forward under the blanket, pull off my shoe and sock, and burrow my naked foot into his hands. He holds my foot, massaging it and running his fingers lightly over my skin. I think I might faint from pleasure.

We ride like that, without talking, until my foot falls asleep and eventually my entire leg goes numb. I pull my leg back and lean forward, resting my head against the back of his seat. He slides his hand under the blanket and our fingers entwine.

We are holding hands. He loves me.

The rest of the day passes in a blur. All the cold, anxious edges of that Midwest winter's day crystallize into pristine happiness. I see and hear nothing but Nathaniel—the sparkle of his blue eyes, the sunshine of his goofy, lopsided grin; even his annoying distractibility seems suddenly endearing.

We secretly hold hands while riding the ski lift. We race each other downhill, laughing uproariously every time I duff a mogul and land on my butt. We eat steaming bowls of soup in the ski lodge, and Nathaniel tells cruel jokes about handicapped people.

I am uncomfortable, but I laugh anyway.

On one of our last rides up the ski lift, Nathaniel takes off a glove and reaches for my hand. He pulls off one of my gloves. "I want to touch skin to skin," he says.

It is snowing lightly, the flakes drifting between us as our hands clasp together. He grins at me. I feel the color burn my cheeks. I want him to say he loves me. Just say it; *say* it!

"So…my grandfather seems to like you," I venture.

"Yeah, he talked to my parents," Nathaniel says. "We gotta keep it quiet for a while, get through high school and everything."

"I'm graduating in a few months. What should I do afterward?"

"Wait for me."

I smile. "Now, why should I do that?"

He glances over his shoulder to make sure we are far from his parents' view and then releases my hand, wraps his arm around me, and scoots close. I shriek as the ski lift wobbles. He laughs. "Don't worry; I got you."

"You got me? For sure?"

"Yeah, I got you, and you should wait for me because I love you."

This is all I want. I lean against the warmth of his body. It is all going to work out fine. I will marry Nathaniel, leave home, and move to Chicago. As long as I have Nathaniel, I can survive a lifetime in The Assembly.

"I love you too," I say.

"That's it. That's the whole story."

I laugh. "And they lived happily ever after?"

"Pretty much, yeah."

We rest against each other in peaceful silence, floating high above the snowy trees.

Two weeks later, Nathaniel sent me a letter. Basically, he said we needed to repent for touching each other. He quoted a Bible verse about confessing sin and being cleansed from all unrighteousness. He ended his letter by saying he was praying for me and asking that I not tell anyone about what had happened between us.

I wrote him back saying yes, of course our relationship must be Christ honoring and that I respected him for obeying the Lord's voice in his life. And…did he still love me?

Nathaniel never wrote back. A month of silence turned into four.

A few weeks before I graduated from high school, I woke up in the middle of the night and couldn't go back to sleep. I grabbed my journal and snuck downstairs to write.

I forced myself to write the words acknowledging that Nathaniel's letter was nothing more than a spiritualized way of breaking up with me. I had defiled our relationship by letting him touch me.

In the years to come, our paths would cross at inter-Assembly gatherings. Nathaniel always pretended he barely knew me.

Chapter 13

Surrendering to God and Man

Mom was acting weird.

Suddenly she was preparing my favorite foods, excusing me from household responsibilities, and encouraging me to take frequent naps. While I did homework, she'd sit on my bed and flip through her house décor catalogs. It was as if she *wanted* to hang out with me.

I was accustomed to Mom's watching my every move and holding me accountable for every infraction, but ever since Nathaniel broke up with me, something was different about the way she watched me. She anticipated my needs. She brought me glasses of cold water, tidied my room, and organized my drawers. She was extraordinarily patient, understanding, and lenient. She *hovered*.

This was such a change I couldn't help but feel wary. What was going on? One afternoon I found out.

Mom calls me to her room and tells me to sit on her bed. "Elizabeth," she begins, "the Lord has told me to tell you something."

I brace myself. Whenever the Lord starts talking to my parents, I get nervous. But this time, I'm not sure what I've done to deserve punishment. Since losing Nathaniel, I've given up everything. I've quit the swim team, stopped hanging out with my friends, and resigned myself to living at home for college. I dress modestly. I go to all the meetings. Isn't it enough?

I look down at my hands. They are trembling.

"Don't worry; you're not in trouble," Mom says.

I clasp my hands together.

"Why are your hands shaking?"

"Oh, I don't know. I've been getting these weird episodes where my body starts shaking for no reason."

"Really?"

"Yeah, and sometimes my stomach gets supertight and I feel really cold. Sometimes I feel my heart racing. Or I get dizzy and feel like I might faint."

Mom's brow furrows, and she sits down beside me and takes my hands. "Elizabeth, I'm worried about you."

I don't know what to say, so I remain quiet. How can she be worried about me when I am doing everything she and Dad want me to do? I am living the life they want me to live. Isn't this "God's best" for me?

"Well, I've been waiting to tell you a story about my life," Mom says. "I think you're old enough now to understand. Did I ever tell you about the man I was engaged to before I met your father?"

I am incredulous. "You were engaged before you met Dad?"

Mom nods. "When I was eighteen, I fell in love with a very kind, wonderful man. We dated for a while, and when he asked me to marry him, I said yes."

I stare at Mom, dumbfounded. "Why haven't you told me this before?"

"Shh," Mom says. "Let me finish, and then you'll understand. We were happily engaged and making our wedding plans when Daniel Wagner—that was my fiancé—became very sick. He was taken to the hospital, and they removed his spleen. But—there were complications, and he was moved to ICU. I visited him every day after school."

Mom's eyes are misting with tears, and she pauses for a moment to wipe them. I watch her quietly.

"One day when I was at school, he had an unexpected heart attack and died. I never had the chance to tell him good-bye. After I heard the news, I went straight to my bedroom and got down on my knees. I said, 'God, if You don't show me right now that You are God, I will not believe in You.' I let my Bible fall open. The words I read were from Isaiah 54. It said God would gather me with great compassion. From that moment on, I knew the Lord was real."

Mom stops and wipes her eyes again. I've never seen my mother cry. She is the epitome of self-restraint. Mom stands and retrieves a tissue. She blows her nose and chuckles a little self-consciously. "All these years later I guess I still get a little sad when I think about Daniel," she says. "It took me months to recover. I used to ride my bike to the cemetery and sit by his grave. I cried so much…"

Mom's voice breaks, and she folds her hands in her lap. She closes her eyes and takes a deep breath. I feel a sudden burst of pity for her. I reach out and hug her. Mom lightly pats my arm. Then she sits up straight and clears her throat.

"I'm all right," she says, suddenly cheerful. "Besides, I learned so much from that experience! I vowed never to love again until the Lord showed me. Now I can see that God was able to take the pain I experienced and draw me into a closer relationship with Him."

"So you joined The Assembly after that?"

Mom nods. "The only thing that gave me comfort in the months after Daniel's death was reading the Bible. I was drawn to your grandfather's preaching because he was so grounded in the Word of God. We really studied our Bibles!"

I shake my head. "I can't believe you've never told me this story!"

"Well, you weren't ready to hear it. I tell you now because I can tell you're unhappy. I wanted to encourage you that even if unfair and difficult things happen to us, God can use these things to bring us into true relationship with Him."

"Sometimes I think it would just be better if I died," I say.

Mom gasps. *"What?"*

"Well, I've given up so much because Dad said it compromised my commitment to The Assembly. I gave up my writing job, my dreams of going away to college. Dad says God comes first in our lives, which means The Assembly comes first."

"But why would that make you want to die? I don't understand."

I fall quiet. I'm not sure I am ready to tell her about the scary thoughts, dreams, and urges I've been having. Suicide, I remember Dad telling me, was the most selfish thing a person could do. I don't want to be selfish. But sometimes I feel as though I would rather die than live the rest of my life completely obedient to The Assembly.

"Elizabeth?"

"I don't know. Being in The Assembly makes me sad. I feel trapped."

Mom thinks about this for a moment. "Well," she says, "what helped me was full surrender. I completely, unequivocally surrendered to God."

"You mean, you surrendered to The Assembly?"

"No, I mean I surrendered to the Lord. Period. No matter where you are, you can always surrender to the Lord."

I think about this. *Maybe she is right. Maybe I'm not surrendered enough. Maybe if I fully surrender, then the dark, the terrible thoughts will stop. Maybe if I completely offer myself as a living sacrifice to God, I will experience the kind of peaceful love I felt when Nathaniel held my hand— except it will be better because it will be for the glory of God.*

I stand up and give Mom a hug. "Thanks for telling me your story."

Mom smiles and says she is praying for me.

I go to my bedroom and climb under the covers. I am shaking again. I tuck my knees into my chest and squeeze shut my eyes. This time I place no conditions on my surrender. I let it all go. I surrender not only to God but also to The Assembly.

"Jesus, Jesus, Jesus," I pray. "I surrender all."

I fasted from boys and poured all my love into God.

I filled my journal with love poems to Jesus, meditations on Scripture, and prayer requests. I stopped listening to secular music and took up practicing piano again. I read my Bible every day and looked for signs of God's reciprocal love.

God reciprocated.

I saw Him in the gentle rains of spring and felt peace settle over my heart when I prayed each morning. After I landed a part-time job that would help me pay for college expenses, I chose to see it as a sign of His providence.

Slowly, I felt the heavy weight of sadness lift from my heart.

Looking back, I see both naiveté and genuine sincerity. I rather foolishly believed a one-time fast would cure all my problems. But this was tempered by my earnest desire to truly know God. I wanted Him to be real for me the way He had been real for my mom. Like her, I wanted to know His gathering me up with great compassion.

For the first time in my life, I was seeking God because I needed God, because I wanted God, because, frankly, I was making a mess of things and reaping only heartache.

I surrendered and surrendered again. I fasted from romance and made Jesus my boyfriend.

This lasted a whole month. Maybe one and a half, if we're counting months with five Sundays. After all, I told myself, fasting wasn't supposed to last *forever*. I reminded God that I'd been honoring Him, and it would be awesome if He honored me back—this time with a real, flesh-and-blood man. I mean, Jesus was a great boyfriend and all, but things were sort of lacking in the kissing department.

I've never seen so many stars.

I prop my head on my arms and gaze up at the inky midnight sky, catching my breath in wonder. All is quiet save the gentle sound of tiny waves slapping the side of our houseboat. The black shadow of a cliff looms behind me, blotting out a rectangle of sky. I sigh deeply and feel myself relaxing into my sleeping bag.

It is the summer after high school graduation, and I've spent the last eight weeks on a mission trip, preaching the gospel and visiting sister Assemblies across the United States. Now I am traveling back to California with my parents and a few Assembly friends.

Dad decided to take a short detour, and we rented a houseboat in Flaming Gorge, Wyoming, for a few days. On the second night of the trip, I climb up to the roof to watch the stars, dragging my sleeping bag behind me. Someone is already there, sitting silently in a beach chair.

"Oh, did you want to be alone?" I ask, squinting through the darkness, unsure about whom I'm disturbing.

"No, I don't want to be alone," says a calm, quiet voice. "Come sit with me."

I recognize the voice as belonging to Matt, one of the few Assembly brothers with whom I feel truly safe. He is calm, steady, and genuinely interested in the well-being of others. Matt is four years older; he'd entered The Assembly his senior year of high school, right after a football injury sidelined his plans for playing at the college level. Despite our starkly different personalities, we'd struck up a friendly rapport over the years.

I roll out my sleeping bag about five feet away from Matt and settle down to gaze at the sky. It is a perfect, clear late-summer evening. After the busyness of summer evangelizing, it feels good to simply slow down and be in nature.

Something about being outdoors soothes my spirit. I feel closer to God, as if His presence is more accessible somehow. The expansiveness of creation gives me hope that God is bigger than I've been taught, bigger than The Assembly, bigger than I've imagined.

I glance over at Matt. He sits very still, his head tipped up to the sky, lips moving in silent prayer. I watch him pray, feeling as if I am eavesdropping on something sacred and private. But I can't look away.

Matt's connection with God is different from mine. Matt has this unwavering, unflustered, quiet confidence about his faith. It provokes in me a kind of godly jealousy: I want what he has. I want that kind of peace.

"The stars are beautiful, aren't they?" Matt says softly.

I turn away, embarrassed. *He must know I was watching him.*

"He tells the number of the stars; He calls them all by name," he says, quoting Psalms.

"I love that verse."

"If God cares enough to call each star by name, imagine how much He must care about us."

I pull my sleeping bag up to my chin and shiver a little. Matt is a man of few words, but when he does speak, his words feed me. I've seen the books he is reading—the poetry of Tennyson, the journals of missionary Jim Elliot, Milton's *Paradise Lost*—and I am inspired.

A year ago, Matt told me he'd switched his college major from engineering to English. It was a risky, impractical, and totally thrilling decision. Matt seems somehow renegade and wild, unpredictable and intense. And yet he has a steady depth of character, an assured internal compass that guides him.

"It's hard for me to believe God cares that much," I confess. "I love the Lord, but I can't ever seem to keep the commitments I make."

Matt says nothing in reply, and for a moment I'm not sure he's heard me. I am about to repeat myself when he starts speaking. "I see the sincerity of your soul, Elizabeth. It is beautiful to me."

I catch my breath, surprised. No one has ever complimented my *soul*. In fact, no man has ever talked to me like this. I am speechless. I've always admired Matt, but I was sure he thought of me as nothing more than an immature little sister. Is it possible he likes me more than that?

"Wow, thanks," I finally say.

"I've always liked you, Elizabeth," he says, turning to face me.

"What?" And then half joking, "I thought you didn't like rebellious women!"

Matt chuckles. "You're spicy, that's for sure."

"I'll take 'spicy.' It's better than rebellious."

"I don't think you're rebellious. I just think you feel things really deeply."

"Well, I probably feel too much," I say. "It brings me a lot of heartache."

"No, no. It's a gift—being able to feel and express those deep things. Ever since I met you, I've admired that."

I'm silenced by surprise. Matt's candor is unexpected, borderline forbidden. In The Assembly, men and women aren't supposed to speak intimately. I think back through my high school years and begin to realize how, during youth group outings, Matt had frequently initiated conversations with me. I've always thought he was just being nice, but now I feel a small thrill. Matt *likes* me.

I've never once considered the possibility that Matt would take romantic interest in me, if only because he seemed so far out of my spiritual league. He is more mature, responsible, and, well, *serious* than I am. I've always assumed he would want a similarly mature, even-tempered spouse. Matt is an even better choice than Nathaniel. With Matt as my husband, life inside The Assembly would not only be bearable, it might even be enjoyable.

I take a deep breath. "Well, I've always admired you, Matt. I know you've been through a lot of pain and disappointment in your life, but it's pretty inspiring the way you've turned that pain into devotion to God."

"Ever since my parents' divorce, I've always told myself I won't settle for anything less than a true soul-relationship. That goes for my relationship with God and with—my future wife, God willing."

"A soul-relationship?" I laugh. "Most brothers in The Assembly want a quiet, submissive little wife."

"Yeah, I'm not interested in that at all," Matt says, laughing. "I'm a strong guy, and I want someone who can challenge and inspire me. That can only happen in an equal partnership."

I drop my voice to almost a whisper. "You could get in trouble for saying that. Don't get me wrong; I love the way you're talking right now—it reminds me of the Matt I used to talk with in high school. But... ever since you moved into that training home last year, I sorta thought I'd lost you—the old you."

Matt shrugs. "I'm just under a lot of pressure. But I'm still the same guy you've always liked."

"You're under a lot of pressure?"

"Yeah. Your dad, your grandfather, Danny, Mark, Rod—all those men in church leadership want something from me. I'm working really hard to do what God wants me to do. But don't distance yourself from me because—well, let's just say I really like you."

In The Assembly, that is practically a declaration of love. I can't contain my delight and burst into laughter. Matt joins me, but only for a moment. He quickly pulls himself together. "I'm probably saying too much," he says. "I should have talked to your dad first."

I shake my head and try to muffle my laughter. "Thanks for saying what you said. I'm honored."

In the silver moonlight, he catches my eye, and we smile at each other. "This fall I was hoping to ask your dad's permission to court you," Matt says. "I mean, if that's okay with you."

Far away in the night, a coyote howls. A breeze from the lake picks up and cools my hot, flushed skin. I look away, grateful for darkness. I'm not ready for Matt to see how his words make me blush.

"It's more than okay." We laugh, the sound of our voices echoing off the canyon walls.

It's the fall of my freshman year in college, and I'm attending the local state university. Since Dad insisted moving away for school was not God's will for me, I've decided that some kind of college education is better than none at all. The only problem is that being at home means I'm still subject to Dad's rules—like attending a single sisters' retreat led by Grandma.

I asked Dad to let me skip it, but he refused, saying as long as I lived in his home, I'd go to these retreats, and anyway, she was my grandmother—where was my respect?

"Besides," Dad said with a wink, "Matt has asked for permission to court you, and since you're in college now, it's high time you learned how to be a biblical, godly wife."

I wanted to say Matt loved me for who I was and had even loved me while I was in the middle of my "rebellious" high school years, but I knew such justifications were futile. Courtship meant attending "biblical womanhood" retreats.

The retreat has hardly begun before I start feeling scared.

I am sitting on the couch, squished between several other "sisters." I nervously smooth my skirt over and over. We all wear long skirts, loose-fitting blouses, and no makeup. At these retreats Grandma insists we leave our blow-dryers, makeup, and other "vain distractions" at home.

To distract myself, I flip through the book we'd been assigned to read ahead of time. It is called *On the Other Side of the Garden* and, from what I can tell, is mainly about the perversity of feminism and how it has destroyed God-given gender roles.

Grandma begins the meeting with prayer, asking the Lord to soften our hearts. Grandma pleads with God to rebuke our wayward spirits, which naturally seek to resist His truth.

As she prays, I get the vague sense she is directing the prayer at me. I can't help but wonder if Dad had briefed Grandma about my character flaws in order to help her know how to direct my "wife training."

I feel a prick of shame creep up my spine, remembering Grandma's penchant for public humiliation. At a recent family breakfast, she'd excoriated me for failing to properly lay the breakfast table. I'd set the table with water glasses but had forgotten the coffee mugs. Grandma stopped the breakfast conversation to inform everyone that my forgetfulness was a sign of poor character.

I clutch my hands in my lap and hope Grandma will refrain from embarrassing me here, at the retreat.

After Grandma's opening prayer, we take turns reading the first chapter. We pause at the end of each paragraph for discussion. Grandma explains that as daughters of Eve, we women are especially prone to deception. Eve's first sin, she explains, was not eating the apple. It was acting outside her role as Adam's helpmeet. She should have stayed by Adam's side at all times. Why was she anywhere near the forbidden tree? Grandma concludes that since all of us are also easily deceived, the only way to prevent our falling into sin is by remaining under the authority of the men in our lives.

We finish the first chapter and break into prayer groups. Grandma assigns her personal assistant, Sister Ruth, as my prayer partner. Sister Ruth is a short, pinched-faced woman who wears the same outfit every day: baggy turtleneck, ankle-length skirt, and orthopedic shoes. She never wears makeup or does anything with her frizzy hair. As we settle into a quiet spot away from the group, Sister Ruth begins by kindly patting my knee.

"Now, you just talk to me like I'm your friend," she says, squinting at me from behind her glasses.

I smile and nod, feeling uneasy. How can I confide in her as if she is my friend when she really isn't? The last time I'd trusted one of Grandma's insiders, I was called into a counseling meeting with Grandma, who just happened to know all my private struggles.

"So, what are your besetting sins?" Sister Ruth asks. "I'd like you to be specific so I know how to pray for you."

I feel my hands begin to tremble. *This is a setup.* Whenever someone in The Assembly asks you to share specific details of your life in order to "pray for you," the request is just a spiritualized way of gleaning personal information, which she then relays to the higher-ups. I know how this works.

I scramble for a response and end up defaulting to a generic sin issue: needing more discipline in my prayer life. Sister Ruth seems disappointed, and for a moment, I almost feel sorry for her. It isn't her fault, really. Women under Grandma's spiritual tutelage often seek ways to earn her approval. If Sister Ruth got the scoop on my intimate sin issues, she'd win points with Grandma. Both Papa and Grandma are fond of loyalty tests, often intentionally pitting people against each other to determine the most devout Assembly member.

After returning to the group for lunch, I find I can't eat. My stomach has hardened into knots. I can't help worrying that by evading Sister Ruth's questions, I'll be accused of stubbornness, pride, and refusing to fully participate.

I look at the food on my plate and feel queasy: a small scoop of boiled brown rice, several strands of roasted asparagus, and a thin slice of baked chicken. Eating a sparse diet is also part of Grandma's spiritual philosophy because it mortifies the flesh. I take one bite of chicken, wash it down with water, and then push the rest of the food around my plate to make it look as if I've eaten.

Grandma begins the second session of the day with more reading. We learn that women functioning outside their God-given roles are guilty of undermining God's eternal plan: in order for God to accomplish His will, men must lead and women must follow. Grandma says that when Eve was created she was made from Adam's rib, and the fact that there is no biblical mention of God breathing life into her, the way He did with Adam, proves that woman's soul is subject to a man's soul. "There are incidents of women usurping male leadership even right here in The Assembly," Grandma says.

Several sisters gasp. Right here? In *our* holy gathering?

Grandma nods solemnly. "Last week when a young sister arrived late to Sunday worship, she refused to sit where the usher led her. Instead, this rebellious young sister asked for a different place."

I feel myself beginning to blush. Grandma is talking about me. I want to explain myself but realize this would come across as defensive, an action Grandma calls "justifying sin." Instead, I bow my head.

What had really happened last week was that the usher led me to the front row, and being nervous about having all eyes on me, I'd quietly asked for a seat farther back. The congregation was singing a hymn and nobody heard me. But still, that action warranted this public rebuke from Grandma.

I feel my blouse turning wet. I keep my eyes firmly planted on the floor as Grandma asks several sisters to share how that rebellious woman could have behaved more biblically.

As soon as the session is over, I bolt to the bathroom. I turn the faucet on full blast and smother my face in the hand towel. I want darkness, nothingness. I chew the edge of the towel, then shove it in my mouth and bite down until my teeth hurt. It isn't enough. The shame lies heavily on me. I pull up my skirt and sit on the toilet. I rake my fingernails across my upper thighs, digging deep lines into my skin.

I scratch until my thighs are covered in angry red marks. I scratch until the pain makes me gasp. I take a deep breath and then feel it: that welcome wash of relief spreading over me, physical pain obliterating mental pain.

I stare at myself in the bathroom mirror and practice smiling. Everything is fine, fine, fine. I am *surrendered*. I am a living sacrifice. I am the oldest granddaughter of George and Betty Geftakys! I am a good example!

Suddenly, my stomach lurches and I dry heave. My hands are shaking. I feel dizzy. *No, no, no. Stop. Control yourself.* I grip the edge of the sink and command my body to obey. But my body refuses, heart racing, palms clammy, my mouth so dry I feel like gagging again.

Oh God, help me. Not another anxiety attack, please.

Like a small point of light, a thought comes to me: *This is your valid excuse. You can tell her you are sick.*

I stumble out of the bathroom and make my way to Grandma. If there is one excuse Grandma accepts, it is illness. She's been on the brink of death my entire childhood. It is why we pray for her every week at the prayer meeting; it is why, Papa says, she rarely attends meetings. Nobody seems to know exactly what is wrong with her, just that she is very frail.

"I…I need to go home," I say. My whole body is quivering. "I almost fainted in the bathroom. I think I've come down with the flu."

Grandma narrows her eyes at me, saying nothing. She folds her hands on her lap and picks at a thumbnail.

"I'm sorry, Grandma," I say. "I have to go."

Grandma nods slightly without looking at me.

I gather my things and hurry out the door before she can say another word. I can hardly get my key in the ignition of my car because my fingers are trembling so badly. I am breathing in short, panicky gasps, and my heart pounds wildly. I finally get the car going and back out of the driveway, away from the single sisters' training home, away from Grandma.

Away, away.

If I want an Assembly-approved courtship with Matt, I realize, I will have to do it The Assembly Way. If I defy my grandmother, she will tell Dad I'm not ready for courtship.

But the most dreadful realization of all is that as a woman, my entire identity is defined by my relationship to men. Being a woman in The Assembly means nothing less than total subjugation.

As I turn the corner, a panicked, guttural sound erupts from my throat. I am screaming in a voice I barely recognize as my own.

Chapter 14

Thought Virgin

In The Assembly, we didn't date. We courted. We didn't fall in love. We followed God's will.

"Follow God's will and the feelings will follow," Dad said, handing me a book called *I Kissed Dating Goodbye*. "And God's will for you is to wait one year before Matt courts you."

I read the book and learned how dating was unbiblical because it was like practicing for divorce. And saving myself for marriage was far more than sexual purity; I was supposed to guard my heart so I didn't commit emotional fornication. In other words, it wasn't enough that I was a physical virgin. I needed to be a heart virgin, a soul virgin, and a thought virgin.

I pretty much needed to be a robot.

Problem: I already had feelings for Matt. Ever since our night on that houseboat in Wyoming, we'd quietly built our relationship. We attended the same college and met in the library to study together. We took walks in the nearby botanical arboretum. When the speakers in my VW Bug fritzed out, Matt installed new ones. When I got sick, he slipped secret notes to me.

One night, after a secret study session in the student union, Matt told me he loved me. Even then we didn't kiss. Matt simply took my hand, and in the light of the moon I watched our fingers gently intertwine.

When we saw each other at Assembly meetings, we spoke in coded language. Matt would casually shake my hand and greet me as he did anyone else. "Hello, Sister Liz. How's the Lord encouraging you?"

"Hi, Brother Matt. I'm reading the book of Ecclesiastes."

"Ecclesiastes" was our code word. Some of our first conversations had been about that book of the Bible, and I'd underlined Ecclesiastes 3:14, "I know that everything God does will remain forever; there is nothing to add to it and there is nothing to take from it" (NASB). I clung to that verse as a promise we'd be together someday.

In order to prove himself worthy of marrying me, Matt had to live in a brothers' training home, receive formal indoctrination into The Assembly, faithfully lead a campus Bible study, serve on summer mission trips, and regularly meet with my grandfather. I had to attend sisters' retreats and learn the biblical guidelines for becoming a submissive wife.

So, for a whole year we pretended to be nothing more than casual friends—at least in public.

During my sophomore year of college, Dad finally gave his permission for us to court. But we had rules. Matt was allowed to take me out for dinner twice a month, and I had to be home by ten o'clock in the evening. We could not hold hands or kiss. We weren't allowed to discuss our future together, and most of all, we weren't allowed to discuss our relationship with anyone but my parents.

We followed almost none of the rules. The tiny margin of freedom we'd been given was like a crack in the dam. Our feelings came pouring out. On our first date, we made out on the beach. On our second date, I took off my shirt. By our third date, we were talking about getting married. We fell in love hard and fast. Six months later (Assembly courtships were always very short), Matt took me to breakfast for my twentieth birthday and pulled an engagement ring out of his pocket.

I said yes.

———

The night before my wedding, I couldn't sleep. I was sick with a chest cold, and I was fretful.

It wasn't just the usual anxiety of a virgin bride that kept me awake. I felt a nameless dread growing inside me. Something had happened to Matt. He had changed during our ten-month engagement. I couldn't help but wonder if the two years he'd spent living in a rigid training home had taken their toll.

Sometimes the kind, soulish Matt morphed into a cold robot I called "Assembly Matt." Assembly Matt was rigid and spoke in a monotone. Assembly Matt wanted to please Assembly leadership.

Whenever Real Matt became Assembly Matt, I became something strange too. I stopped speaking directly. I hinted, I suggested, I pointed out problems I saw in The Assembly with the hope he'd see the sickness in my family and the church. But instead, I just drove him crazy because, despite our genuine affection for each other, it seemed as though we were frequently at cross-purposes.

We began arguing. He said I was too emotional. I said he was too harsh and controlling.

One night after an impossible argument where he rebuked me for once again questioning The Assembly, I took off my engagement ring and threw it on the ground. I said it was over. But the next morning I apologized, and Matt slid the ring back on my finger. My biggest hope was that when we married, we could finally start a life of our own. Moving out of our respective training homes and into our own private apartment would give us a chance to rediscover the people we had been when we fell in love. I told myself all we needed was some freedom and privacy.

Ours was to be a huge Assembly wedding with over five hundred guests from all over the country. To accommodate everyone, we'd rented the biggest hall in the student union at Cal State Fullerton. Papa George and Dad both insisted on preaching.

Assembly weddings were considered serious church services with hymns and a sermon. We didn't hire a caterer, a band, or a DJ. The women in our training home baked and cooked our wedding food.

I finally get up at three in the morning and go downstairs to make myself tea. I sit on a kitchen bar stool and stare out at the dark, rainy morning. In less than twelve hours, I'll be Mrs. Matthew Henderson. Part of me is excited; part of me is terrified.

I am about to go back upstairs to bed when Dad enters the kitchen. "Can't sleep, eh, Wiz?"

"Not really."

"Well, that's understandable. It's a big day. For all of us."

I watch Dad shuffle around the kitchen. He drinks a glass of water and eats a slice of cheese from a plate that has been prepared for the wedding reception. His eyes are bloodshot, and his hair is a mess. He sniffs around the fridge for another minute before turning to look at me. "Now, Wiz, I'm probably gonna cry a bit during the wedding."

"That's okay."

"I love you and am believing God's best for you."

"I know."

"No, Wiz. I'm serious."

"I believe you, Dad."

"I know this courtship thing was hard on you, but you were only eighteen when Matt asked to court you, so we needed you to wait."

I nod.

Dad roots through the cupboards and pulls out a box of crackers. I watch him eat, remembering all the times he's tried to lose weight. He's never succeeded. Dad has been obese since I was a kid, and no matter how many times Papa George hounds him about it, Dad can't stay away from the fridge. "Bodily exercise profiteth little," Dad likes to say, quoting 1 Timothy 4:8, "but godliness is profitable unto *all* things!"

Dad returns to the fridge and eyes the bounty of food for my reception. "This is gonna be a glorious day for the Lord," he says with a chuckle. Dad winks at me and grabs a cluster of grapes. He pops the grapes into his mouth and shuffles back to the kitchen counter. He slaps me on the back. "God's gonna do a great work today!"

I nod. Wedding days are not about the couple being married. They are about giving a Christian witness to the world. Everything from the drinks served (only fruit punch) to the bride's dress (fully modest) to the music played (only hymns or approved Christian songs) is carefully scrutinized for its ability to bring glory to God.

I push back from the counter. "Well, I'm going back up to bed."

"Okay, sweetie. I love you."

"You too."

But I can't sleep. I am coughing pretty badly from a cold I caught just a few days earlier. My nose is stuffy and my sinuses ache. I know I should feel happy—this is my wedding day, after all!—but all I feel is sick and worried.

After another hour of tossing around, I finally realize I'm not going to sleep. I get out of bed and slip into the shower. I shave my legs, thinking, *This is the last time I'll shave my legs as a virgin.*

For days I've been thinking things like this. *This is the last time I'll do laundry…as a virgin. This is the last time I'll cook a meal…as a virgin.* I wonder if, after my wedding night, people will look at me and know I'm not a virgin anymore. I've been taught that sex is such a huge deal, such a monumentally life-altering experience that I fully expect it to change everything about me, even my appearance.

I emerge from the shower, towel off, and try to avoid looking at myself in the mirror. Will sex help me finally start liking my body? What would it feel like not to be ashamed and disgusted by my physical being? I can't even imagine. The Assembly's strict modesty rules are intended to protect my dignity and purity. But for me, the strictness turned into a kind of negative hyperawareness of my body. All I see are flaws. I weigh barely one hundred twenty pounds, but when I look in the mirror, I think I look fat. I scrutinize every inch of my body for imperfection.

I hate my hourglass shape because if I don't cover it properly, I am responsible for leading men into lust. I am terrified about being naked in front of Matt. I look at my perfectly pedicured toes and remember, with dismay, the words of my roommate:

"Honey, I'm pretty sure the *last* thing he'll be looking at are your toes."

Couldn't we just have sex in the dark?

Downstairs, Mom is making oatmeal. I settle myself at the counter and tell her I feel nauseous. She insists I eat the special oatmeal she's making because I need my energy.

I eat a few bites. And then run to the bathroom. I vomit. I can't believe this is happening on my wedding day. I go back upstairs and crawl into my parents' bed. I am shaking all over.

An hour before the photographer arrives, Mom shakes me gently by the shoulders and says it is time to get dressed. I am still nauseous and getting more anxious with each passing moment.

Mom helps me into my huge petticoat and then tells me to lift my arms so she can lower the wedding gown over my head.

We'd found my wedding dress on an As Is rack at a bridal salon. It was long-sleeved with a modestly cut neckline. Mom wanted to know why it was on clearance. The saleslady told us long-sleeved wedding gowns were not popular sellers, and Mom shook her head sadly. "How tragic." Mom sighed. "It's a shame immodesty is so fashionable." The salon attendant just looked confused.

But even this gown wasn't modest enough. Mom said the train was too long and the back of the dress was too low. However, since it was a floor model, it was a good price and Mom bought it. She had a friend shorten the train and use the excess fabric to sew a panel that covered my upper back. In the end, I am swathed head to toe in yards and yards of cream-colored dupioni silk.

"Shouldn't I be wearing pure white since I'm a virgin?" I ask, worried that Grandma Geftakys might disapprove.

"There were no pure-white dresses on sale," Mom says. That settles it.

I stand still as my mom and sister dress me. Jacqueline, a little girl who is living with our family at the time, peeks around the bedroom door and asks to help. My fingers are trembling too much to fasten the buttons on my sleeves, so I nod at Jacqueline, and she does it for me.

I glance at my best friend, Jael, who has flown in for the wedding. She stands at the mirror in my bedroom, dabbing liquid foundation on her face and watching me out of the corner of her eye. Once I am fully dressed, Mom goes downstairs to check on the photographer, and I swish my way over to Jael. "I feel awful," I whisper.

"I'm pretty sure it's normal to feel nervous on your wedding day," she says, dabbing at my lips with a tissue. "You need more lip gloss."

"It's not just nerves."

Jael pauses, her dewy blue eyes locking with mine. "Say the word and I'll bust you out of here." She is dead serious.

I grip her hand, shaking my head. "I'm so scared."

Jael leans in close, her lips next to my ear. "Does Matt really love you? I mean, does he love you *for you*?"

"I think so," I whisper. "And I love him. But there's so much extra pressure on us... And he's been acting so strict ever since living in that training home."

Jael nods soberly. She has been in and out of The Assembly for the past two years, struggling to stay in college, fleeing to her grandparents' house in Arizona, chopping off all her hair, smoking cigarettes. Both Dad and Matt say I should withdraw my friendship from her. But I can't. I trust her.

"Well, I love you no matter what," Jael says and hugs me. "Except I kind of also hate you right now."

"What? Why?"

"Because you're sick as a dog, and you still look so pretty!"

This makes me laugh. "Yeah, well. At least you have boobs. I can't even fill out the top of my wedding dress!"

Jael snickers. "We have a little sister, and she hath no breasts," she says, quoting Song of Solomon. She pulls four tissues from the Kleenex box. "Here, stuff your bra."

I ball up the tissues and stick them inside my bra. Jael snorts with laughter when I need more. "We should just call you 'Grapes of Wrath,'" she says.

I burst into laughter, and for a moment, the tension eases.

The rest of the day passed in a blur.

Papa George and Grandma arrived for pictures. Papa was in high spirits, yelling "Praise the Lord!" all over the place, bursting into spontaneous hymn singing, and regaling everyone with stories. He and Dad bantered back and forth, laughed, slapped shoulders, shouted hallelujahs. As usual, Grandma was silent and unsmiling.

Papa George and Dad both preached at the wedding, rambling on for over an hour. Dad cried while he dictated our marriage vows, and Papa boomed "amen" from the first row. There were hundreds of guests to greet, most of whom I didn't know.

At the end of the day, as the last guests are finally leaving the reception, I can remember only one thing: when Matt saw me coming down the aisle, he wept.

I'd never seen him cry. Assembly Matt rarely showed emotion of any kind. But as soon as I saw his tears, I tucked them away in my heart. *His tears are proof of love,* I tell myself. *No matter what happens, remember that underneath The Assembly, we have real love. We are real people.*

The moment we are alone together, riding an elevator up to the hotel room where we will spend our first night together, Matt turns to me and a huge smile breaks over his face.

"We made it!" he says. "We finally made it!"

I look into his eyes and see no trace of Assembly Matt. I see only love. I fling my arms around his neck with relief. Matt wraps his arms around me and holds me close, lifting me off the floor. "Did you really worry, my bride?" he asks, pressing his lips to my ear.

I nod against his shoulder.

"You don't have to worry or doubt any longer," he says. "I'll always love you. I'll never leave you."

I tuck my head against his shoulder as we exit the elevator and walk to our hotel room. Matt carries me over the threshold and gently lays me down on the bed.

The next morning when I look in the mirror, the first thing I see is my smile.

Chapter 15

The Selfer's Prayer

"Get down on your knees and repent," Grandma Geftakys says, her voice quiet and fully controlled.

I kneel on Grandma's bedroom floor and glance at Matt. He won't look at me. We've been married for only six months, but whenever we're around my family, it seems as though Matt switches back to being Assembly Matt. And this time I'm in trouble with my family.

Grandma called this meeting because I was asking too many questions. Uncle David was still preaching and being financially supported by The Assembly, even though he continued beating my cousins and aunt. I wanted to know why. Uncle David had beaten my cousin Rachel so severely she'd lost partial hearing in one ear and a judge had granted her a restraining order against him. I asked why this wasn't being addressed.

Dad and Papa George told me to mind my own business. I kept asking. That's when Papa George told Matt he needed to bring me to Grandma Betty for rebuke.

"Say the Selfer's Prayer," Grandma commands. "Admit your life is a failure and a mess."

We'd been required to memorize the Selfer's Prayer during a recent Assembly workshop. I struggle to begin, my voice a whisper. "Father...I admit that I'm a selfer...and have been struggling in my own resources to live the Christian life. I confess that my life is a failure and a mess. I now give up my life and affirm with You my death with Christ. I also affirm that I have risen with Christ and am seated in Him in the heavenly places. I give You complete control of myself and everything I'm hanging on to, to meet my needs. Do with me whatever You choose. I now thank You that Christ is my life."

"You didn't pray that like you meant it," Grandma says. "You're going to stay on your knees and pray this prayer until you're fully contrite."

A wave of panic shoots up my spine, and I grasp the edge of the chair where I am kneeling. I will myself not to faint. I look to Matt for help, but he is kneeling at another chair, his head bent in prayer.

I know what is required during these rebuke sessions. Grandma wants a full, complete breaking. Grandma wants me to confess everything. She has been leading up to this moment over the past few weeks, calling me in for weekly appointments where she plotted my "sin patterns" on charts and made me pray long prayers on the wood floor. Once she had me march around the room while she named my sins and proclaimed victory over them. She kept me marching—"like we're bringing down the sinful walls of Jericho!"—until she was convinced I had fully repented.

After each appointment with Grandma, I am a mess. I've begun hurting myself again. Using the sharp edge of the diamond on my wedding ring, I carve bloody crosses into my upper thighs. I hide the marks beneath my modest skirts and don't let Matt see me naked. I am also losing weight and going strangely numb.

I rarely ask direct questions. In fact, my questions about Uncle David are some of the only direct inquiries I've made. I never make declarative statements. I speak *around* sensitive topics instead of about them. I pad my concerns with all kinds of verbal equivocation, cute little chirps, noises, clucking, "uptalking." I finish my sentences in a singsong voice.

This way of talking is common among Assembly women. We've been trained—if only by group imitation—to speak with a submissive cadence in our voices. This is supposed to give the impression that we are living inside our God-given gender roles and not "speaking like men."

I know that women who speak directly or confidently are often accused of living outside their roles as women. Women are followers, and our deferential speech is supposed to match our roles.

I never tell Matt that my appointments with Grandma are making me feel so terrible because I know he is under intense pressure too. He's working a part-time sales job that just barely makes ends meet so he can be more available for serving in The Assembly. Dad and Papa George are grooming him for full-time ministry by having him preach at campus Bible studies all over Southern California and inviting him to a special leaders' conference.

But there is a problem: me. I don't want to go into full-time ministry in The Assembly. I don't want to move somewhere and plant a new church. I want a "normal Assembly life," which means a life outside leadership. But this frustrates Matt—he really wants to become a full-time pastor. It also frustrates my grandparents, who can't understand why I'm being rebellious and asking all these questions about Uncle David.

Grandma stands over me and taps my shoulders so I bend even farther over the chair. "Your husband's frustration is understandable," she says. "You have not submitted yourself to his leadership. I want you to kneel here until you are fully submitted to your husband."

I clutch the edge of the chair. I fight it. But it is inevitable.

I am breaking. Again. I am surrendering. Again.

I pray until Grandma is satisfied. She thinks I am weeping for my sins, but I am weeping because I finally realize that I will never be free. I see life stretched in front of me, and I weep for all the dreams I'll never fulfill and for the children I will bring into this oppression. I weep for naively hoping my marriage could be different from all the other marriages in The Assembly.

I have already asked around and heard stories from wives facing similar difficulties. One husband banned the word *no* from his wife's vocabulary, claiming she'd never have a justifiable reason for refusing his requests. Another husband set up a "submission test." He gave his wife intentionally convoluted driving directions to see whether she'd obey his leadership or take a driving shortcut. I'd met a wife whose husband wanted her to lose weight, and so he forbade her from eating sweets. When she snuck a bite of ice cream, he sat her down at the table and forced her to eat the entire gallon. She ate until she vomited.

This is biblical marriage. Even the natural affection I feel for Matt is breaking under the strain. I don't want to let go of our love—that pure, beautiful core of love I'd seen in him. Is it possible Matt doesn't see our love anymore? Is it possible he doesn't see *me*? Or us? He sees only the roles we'd been given to play.

I have been given a role to play. My marriage will be an Assembly marriage. There is no other way.

Our husbands are God to us.

The Women's Center at Cal State Fullerton is quiet and empty when I walk in. The woman behind the desk looks just a little older than I am. She smiles and looks up expectantly. I shift my backpack and glance around.

Has anyone from The Assembly seen me come in here? According to Dad, a Women's Center is a pit full of godless feminists. But after my breaking session with Grandma, I am desperate for help. Even from godless feminists.

"I need a safe place to stay," I say softly, leaning close to the desk. My heart is pounding.

The receptionist stands up quickly, as if she's been trained for situations just like mine. "Oh! Okay!" She smiles reassuringly and leads me into a nearby office. Another, older woman smiles and gestures toward a chair, nodding encouragingly at me. It is such a small gesture, offering a chair, but it touches me, and tears well up in my eyes.

"I don't really know why I'm here."

"Well, my name is Ann, and I'm here to help you," the woman says, offering a tissue box.

I blow my nose and wipe my eyes.

"Are you being abused?" Ann asks gently.

"I don't know," I say. *Abuse* seems like such a heavy word. "Maybe? Probably not. No. I don't know."

"What are some of the things you're experiencing?" Ann asks.

I give Ann some examples, including the recent repentance session with my grandma. I watch Ann's face change from mild inquisitiveness to open concern. She reaches across her desk and places her hand on mine. "I don't know a lot about abusive churches," she says. "But it sounds like you're in a scary situation."

It is the first time anyone has validated my experience. Ann gives me words for it. Yes, it is scary. The Assembly is a scary situation.

"I really love my husband," I explain. "We had something real. But… but we're stuck in this church environment…"

"Is he willing to leave the church for you?"

"No."

"Do you have anywhere to go? Maybe other family members or friends?"

"All my family and friends are in the church," I answer. "I have extended family somewhere—but I haven't seen them in so long I don't know where they live."

"Are you not allowed to have friends outside the church?" Ann asks.

I shake my head and start crying again. "I'm sorry about all this crying! Usually I'm much more self-controlled!"

"You don't have to apologize for anything," Ann says. She reaches for an address book on her desk and flips through it. "I know a women's shelter where you can stay for a while."

I feel my heart lurch. *A shelter?*

Ann places a call while I fretfully twist a tissue in my lap. A few moments later she tells me there is a spot available at a place about twenty minutes away.

"You'll need to drive to the Irvine police department so a police escort can take you to the shelter," she says. I nod, my hands shaking. I can't believe how kind she is being with me. I haven't done anything to earn it. Despite what I've been told about godless feminists, this one is nicer to me in five minutes than my own grandma has been to me my entire life.

I get in my car and drive home. Our tiny one-bedroom apartment is empty, but I know Matt will be home soon. It is a church meeting night, and I am expected to have dinner on the table by five thirty. I hurriedly pack clothing, toiletries, and my school supplies. I don't care about bringing much else with me. We don't have fancy things anyway. The heaviest things I carry are my college textbooks. No matter how crazy my life is becoming, I don't want to quit college.

I scribble a note for Matt and leave it on the kitchen counter. I throw my things in the back of my car and drive away. It is a lovely fall afternoon, a perfect day for pumpkin patches and hot apple cider. It doesn't seem like a day for leaving everything I know.

The policemen who escort me are gentle and professional. They lead me to the shelter and wait until I am safely parked behind the locked gates. A door buzzes and I am allowed inside.

The shelter is a cluster of unmarked condos protected by locking gates, security cameras, and an on-site staff. I am welcomed and led to my room without being asked many questions. The room is neat and clean. I share the condo with a mother and her three children, but I have my own room and bathroom. I set my things down on the bed and bury my head in my hands. My thoughts are scrambled and chaotic.

You are sinning against God. You are shaming the Geftakys family. You are ruining everything. You are rebellious. You will be punished for this.

I wander downstairs in a haze, and a therapist invites me into a comfortable sitting room. She sits in a big upholstered chair and smiles at me. I crumple onto the couch.

"Can I call my mom?" I ask.

"Sure, no problem. Would you like me to leave the room so you can have some privacy?"

I nod.

The therapist gets up to go, but I stop her. "Wait!"

"What is it?"

"Do I have to stay here?" I ask. "I mean, are you locking me in here?"

"You came here voluntarily; you can leave at any time," the therapist says, smiling gently.

"I think I need to leave!"

"You just got here, sweetie. Why not stay the night and see how you feel in the morning?"

"I know I just got here but…but…" How am I supposed to explain that leaving my husband means leaving God? How do I articulate the entire self-contained atmosphere of The Assembly? How do I even begin to find the words to say that just being here is a sin?

"Take your time, honey. Call your mom. We can talk again in a few minutes."

I call home. Mom answers on the first ring. "Hi, Mom, it's Elizabeth."

"Where are you?" she shrieks.

I've never heard my mother raise her voice. Mom is always in complete control of her emotions—except for that time she told me about her deceased fiancé. If Mom is freaking out, it means Matt has called home and told my parents I am gone.

"I'm at a safe place," I say.

"What? Where?"

In the background I can hear Dad demanding to talk to me.

"I'm leaving The Assembly."

"No, you're not, Elizabeth," Mom says sternly. She has regained her composure. "You go home right now."

"No, I'm not going home. I'm leaving because Grandma—"

"Don't complain to me about your godly grandmother!" Mom interrupts. "You know better than to run away. This is not how we solve our problems. You are bringing shame on this family and—"

I can hear Dad whispering something to Mom.

"And we will not speak to you until you return home!"

I hang up. The therapist returns a few moments later. I sit stiffly on the couch, staring into space. The voices in my head are shouting at me. Everything is shutting down except the voices. I am going to hell. I am a terrible, wicked sinner.

"I have to go!" I say, bolting upright.

"Okay, honey," the therapist says kindly. "You can come back later if you need to."

I am shaking all over. I dart past her and reach for the door.

"Elizabeth," she says very quietly. I turn toward her. "Did you know that women living in abusive situations try to leave home many, many times before they succeed?"

I hold her eyes for a moment and then run upstairs. I grab my things and race to my car. I can't hear anything but the fear screaming through my body. Staying at the women's shelter seems like a permanent decision. I can't do it. I am going to be one of those women—the ones who go back home. I tear out of the parking lot and drive toward Pacific Coast Highway with all the windows down.

I need to see the ocean, need to smell the salty air. I blast the music and let the wind whip my hair into a wild tangle. On the radio, Alanis Morissette is roaring my pain.

"I'm sad but I'm laughing, I'm brave but I'm chicken shit, I'm sick but I'm pretty, baby."

Why couldn't I just *leave*? Why did I keep going back? Why didn't I speak up more? Why did I remain silent when I knew so many children—my own cousins!—were being beaten? How could I stay in The Assembly?

These questions have plagued me for years. The only answer I have is that a threefold cord held me tightly in place: The Assembly was my faith, my family, and my friends. Leaving The Assembly was like leaving an entire way of life.

When church is *everything*, leaving feels like a horrible, unimaginable divorce. We feel as if we're abandoning our homeland and entering another culture as an immigrant. We have no friends, no outside contacts. We think and speak differently.

In other words, things have to get really bad before we'll leave voluntarily.

Even though I lived in urban Southern California and could have left easily and made a new life for myself—I didn't *feel* as though I could leave. The chains that held me in The Assembly were stronger than iron.

Eventually, it became easier to stay than to go. It was crazy, but at least it was *my* crazy.

I probably would have stayed in The Assembly for my whole life. But I became a mother. And becoming a mother saved me.

Suddenly, I was no longer fighting for myself—I was fighting to save my children.

Chapter 16

Will the Cycle Be Unbroken?

Our baby girl is turning one, and I am already pregnant with a second child.

Mom throws a big family birthday party at her home. Papa George and Grandma attend, as do several visiting missionaries and the women living in my parents' training home. Mom makes pot roast and baked potatoes with gravy. After dinner, everyone gathers in the living room for cake and coffee.

Papa sits on the couch and says he'd like to see Matt's Bible. Before we were married, Matt studied the New International Version of the Bible, but on our wedding day he was given a custom-bound King James Version and told it was time he "matured out of the NIV."

Papa George is partial to the KJV, and he eyes Matt's Bible carefully, smoothing the gilt, wide-margin pages and admiring the soft leather binding. Matt sits next to him, explaining why he chose this particular edition. It is a Bible printed by Cambridge University Press—the gold standard of KJVs—and Papa George nods approvingly.

I sit on the floor with my baby girl, Jewel, and help her open birthday gifts. Jewel is especially delighted with a musical Noah's ark and giggles happily. From the corner of my eye, I notice Grandma watching us closely.

Jewel eventually tires of the presents and, just learning to walk, wobbles toward the coffee table. I catch her hands and ease her away from the sharp corners of the table. Jewel spots a small bowl of chocolates on the table and reaches for it. I tell her not to touch it and move the chocolate outside her reach.

"Oh, don't take the chocolate away!"

Startled, I glance up. Grandma is gesturing at me to move the bowl back to its original place. "Keep the chocolate in front of her. This is a perfect opportunity to test her obedience."

The room falls silent. In a group, Grandma usually remains quiet and simply watches everyone. But when she does speak, everyone is expected to listen.

"You need to purposely cross Jewel's will," Grandma explains, scooting forward on the couch. "You should set up little temptations to test her obedience."

I feel all eyes swivel toward me. Heat flows up my spine, and it is suddenly difficult to breathe. I watch my hand, as if in slow motion, slide the bowl of chocolates back within Jewel's reach. I know it's pointless to look to Matt for help—it's very clear who is in charge here: Grandma Betty.

My daughter's birthday party is no longer a celebration. It is a child-training session. This is how The Assembly ensures its children grow up obedient. Even the simplest circumstance or exchange can be turned into a test. As in my childhood, delayed obedience is disobedience, and hard spankings are the consequence for every infraction. This is how I was raised. Now, Grandma is testing me with my own child. The cycle has come full circle.

Jewel reaches for the chocolate again. "No touch," I say, my voice trembling.

Jewel pauses and looks at me with her big blue eyes. There are bits of cake in her blond curls and a smidge of frosting on the little dimple in her chin. *Please, baby girl, don't touch it.*

Jewel looks back at the chocolate and then grabs the bowl.

Grandma sucks breath through her teeth. "Oh, my, my, Jewel. You just disobeyed your mother!"

Is that excitement I hear in her voice?

Nobody says a word. Mom stands frozen nearby with a cup of creamer in one hand and a bowl of sugar in the other. Dad sits upright in his armchair, nervously bouncing one leg.

I know what I'm supposed to do. My mother has written pamphlets on child-training and held training sessions in this very living room. When I was seventeen, The Assembly started following the child-training methods of Michael and Debi Pearl. We ordered their books by the boxful. I'd attended several young mothers' meetings where we were taught how to implement the spankings. I knew that I was supposed to spank my daughter until, in the words of Michael Pearl, I had "totally defeated" her.

"I'll go get you a paddle," Mom says, setting the sugar and cream on the coffee table.

I gather Jewel in my arms and look over at Grandma. She is suddenly animated. Her eyes gleam, and she is nodding at me.

A wave of dizziness washes over me. I steady myself on the edge of the couch and glance at Matt for help. But his eyes are fixed firmly on his open Bible, and Papa George has already gone back to chatting casually—as if nothing is amiss.

Mom emerges from the kitchen and hands me a wooden cooking spoon. I carry Jewel out of the living room and toward the downstairs guest bathroom. I close the door behind me, flip on the exhaust fan, and crank the faucet full blast. I need the noise to muffle my own cries. I close the toilet lid and lower myself onto it, holding Jewel against me.

She stares up at me, smiling and innocently unaware of what is happening. It is her first birthday. She is my baby, and I am doing this to her. I am training her the way I've been trained. Indeed, to break her will, I'd begun spanking Jewel at six months old.

Oh, God. Help me. Help me now. I wait, the tears still coursing down my cheeks.

And there it is. A small shift. The tiniest point of light breaking through my darkness. It is revelation. *You don't have to break your daughter the way you were broken.*

The force of this realization crashes over me like a wave. It pins me down, helpless. How can I do this? How can I hurt my daughter in the exact same way I'd been hurt? Am I powerless to stop this cycle?

No.

The word I am forbidden to say bursts in my mind like a fireworks explosion. *NO!*

You are not powerless.

I have a choice. I can choose something different. I suddenly remember Dad's words when he was teaching me to surf. If you get wiped out, don't resist the ocean. Wait.

I wait.

Open your eyes.

I open my eyes.

Look for the light.

I look at my daughter, the light of my life.

Kick your way up to the light.

I bury my head in her sweet-smelling curls and kiss her. I kiss her again and again. I can't spank her.

I won't spank her.

I will choose something different. I choose life. I choose freedom.

I kiss my way up to the light.

———

I wish I could say I never spanked my daughter after that. The truth is, I spanked her many more times and often too harshly. That moment in the bathroom *was* a turning point—but it took a couple more years of similar situations before I finally ceased disciplining her in the way I'd been taught. To this day, one of my deepest regrets is that Jewel's earliest years were often marked by punishing spankings. I missed out on some precious bonding time with her because I was so consumed with needing to raise her according to Assembly standards. At the time, I didn't know another way.

Eventually, Matt and I both agreed the discipline methods we'd learned in The Assembly were harmful. We still didn't leave The Assembly, but we began doing things differently.

I am breast-feeding my second baby in the dark. It is early morning. Matt is reading his Bible, and Jewel is still asleep. The phone starts ringing.

"Turn on the news," Matt's best friend, Enoch, says. "Planes are crashing into buildings."

We turn on the radio just as the first tower falls. The phone rings again.

"Turn on the radio," Dad says. "America is under attack."

"Do you think this is war?" I ask.

"It's more than war. It's the End of the World. Jesus is coming soon."

We still don't have a television, so we knock on a neighbor's door. I scream as the second tower falls. My babies start crying.

I go back home. I can't watch any more. I make toast for Jewel. Matt quietly prepares for work with the radio turned low.

"Can't you stay home today?" I ask. "One of those planes was headed here, to Los Angeles."

"They're grounding all the planes," he says and kisses me good-bye.

"We're a one-income family. I have to work. Go to your mom's if you get scared."

The phone rings. Dad again. "Four planes hijacked. Pentagon hit. Pray, Elizabeth. Pray to be made holy during these last days."

In the weeks and months that followed, The Assembly was racked by apocalypse hysteria. Papa George preached that the 9/11 attacks were a true sign that The End was near. Another full-time pastor in The Assembly said he'd heard from God that a nuclear attack on Los Angeles was imminent. He packed up his family and fled to Arizona.

Another Assembly member cashed out his 401(k) because he was convinced Jesus's return was imminent. And when Dad told me I shouldn't attend my college graduation because it was a waste of time, I knew he'd caught the apocalypse fever again. After all, commencement ceremonies didn't matter when the world was going up in smoke. Better to use the time more wisely. Like for praying and evangelizing.

It had taken me seven years to get my degree in English. I'd taken classes part time between babies and Assembly meetings. When I finally finished, I was so proud of myself. Despite all the stress in The Assembly, I'd still achieved a dream.

Even so, I skipped my graduation ceremony. After all, Dad said it was a waste of time.

"Surprise," I say and hold out the pregnancy test.

Matt leans close. "Another baby?" It is less than a year after 9/11, and I am pregnant again.

I'm usually overjoyed about a new baby, but this time all I can feel is exhaustion.

Matt sinks down on the bed next to me and runs a hand over his scruffy cheeks. "Whoa." He sighs. "That'll be what? Three babies in three and a half years?"

"Yeah. Jewel will be three when this new baby is born."

Matt takes my hand and squeezes it. He tips my face up to look into his eyes. "I know this baby is a surprise. But I still believe all babies, no matter when or how they arrive, are precious gifts from God."

"I believe that too. I'm just...my body is breaking down. You see that, right?"

Matt wraps his arms around me, pressing my head against his chest and twining my hair around his fingers. I've continued to have anxiety attacks—although we still don't call them that. We call them "exhaustion." But they happen so frequently that Matt can no longer deny the toll our Assembly lifestyle is taking on me.

Being a mother in The Assembly means back-to-back pregnancies because we are "strongly encouraged" to avoid contraception. Motherhood also means attending four to five weekly meetings, providing hospitality to frequent visitors, and participating in evangelistic outreaches.

"You're right," Matt says. "If we go on with all these meetings and outreaches...well, I feel like I'm going to lose you."

I nod against his chest.

Since 9/11, things in The Assembly have grown only more stressful and chaotic. The Geftakys family is coming undone right in front of everyone. Despite flimsy efforts by Assembly leadership to stop him, my Uncle David has continued beating my aunt. One day, she simply runs away. Nobody knows where she is or how to contact her. My cousins are scattered, people are asking questions, and still my grandparents refuse to talk about it.

Something has to give.

And then it does.

PART
THREE

Chapter 17

A Break That Heals

M att and I decided to stop running from the truth and instead to go on a hunt for it.

Our first source was a website set up by a former Assembly member. We found eyewitness accounts detailing all the ways my grandparents had covered up the abuse in our own family and in The Assembly. We followed up the information from the website with days of research and phone calls. It was difficult and time consuming. Every call was torture—people were terrified of talking, and we were in equal parts beset by doubts and disgusted by what we confirmed.

But that hunt proved to be a turning point for us. We were finally willing and prepared to stop kneeling to The Assembly and the man who ran it and start standing up for a life we believed in.

It is January 2003, just a few weeks away from my third child's birth, when we walk up to my grandparents' house and ring the doorbell for the last time.

We've told Mom and Dad we're doing this. Dad shook his head and stared at the ground. "Just treat them respectfully," he said, sounding defeated.

Mom's face was pale, and she looked as if she might cry. She hugged me. "I love you," she whispered. "I don't want you to leave, but I think I understand why you have to."

It is chilly outside, and I try to wrap my sweater a little closer around my hugely pregnant belly. I glance up at the hand-painted sign above the door: *Jehovah Shalom, The Lord Our Peace.* Papa George likes to say his household is a place of peace. This is also true of The Assembly, he says—our identifying characteristic is unity. But at long last I know how he achieves that kind of unity: by crushing anyone who disagrees with him.

Matt and I are here to confront my grandparents. We know they are covering up Uncle David's abuse while still supporting him through Assembly tithes. What we don't know for sure—but definitely suspect—is that there are other abuses going on in the leadership too: misuse of tithe monies, for example, and adulterous affairs. But for now, we're here to confront Papa George about Uncle David's abuse.

The door opens, and a woman wearing an old apron stands aside to let us enter. I recognize her face—she attends another Assembly in California—but I can't remember her name. We step inside and stand in the unlit foyer.

"I'll go tell Brother George you're here," the woman says softly. "He…uh…he said for you to wait here until he comes downstairs."

I glance at Matt, catching his eye. If Papa George wants us to stand here until he comes downstairs, I'm sure he already suspects something is amiss. I feel a sudden stab of doubt. *What if we are wrong?*

I look at Matt and the stack of papers he holds in his hand. Maybe we don't have the full, conclusive story. But we certainly have enough. We have decided that if Papa and Grandma Betty refuse to tell the truth, we are leaving The Assembly for good. But deep inside, I'm hoping they'll confess everything. I don't want to stay in The Assembly, but it's also the only life I've ever known. Maybe if Papa George and Grandma Betty come clean, we can change things in The Assembly, get back to how things were in the beginning, all fresh and new...

The house, usually bustling with eager acolytes who serve in my grandparents' ministry, is eerily quiet. The guest room on the right is empty.

A door opens upstairs, and we hear footsteps in the hall. Then Papa George charges down in his usual fashion with Grandma following silently behind him. Papa greets us jovially, pounding backs, pumping hands, and bestowing exuberant, sloppy kisses on our cheeks. I turn to Grandma, who leans forward for a brief hug, awkwardly patting my shoulders with her hands while keeping her body away from my pregnant belly.

"My darling!" Papa George says and wraps a thick arm around my shoulders. He leads us down a hall decorated with paintings, placards, and artifacts from his worldwide travels and into the living room.

Ever since I was about ten, Papa George has traveled the world preaching the gospel and planting Assemblies. He is gone nine months of each year. I wonder now if his prolonged absences are to blame for how things are falling apart. People are leaving. People are asking questions. The more Papa George remains silent, the more confusion grows. And all the while, the website written by former Assembly members continues to publish increasingly credible and up-to-the-moment reports.

We settle ourselves on the antique sofa in the formal living room. Papa George's extralarge black Bible is already waiting on the coffee table. Grandma sits in a straight-backed chair, and Papa George sits in a chair next to her, leaning forward a little on his knees, eyes bright with expectation. He seems completely at ease, in command of the situation—as always. I prop a small pillow behind my back and try to get as comfortable as my pregnant belly will allow.

"Shall we begin with prayer?" Papa asks. "Matt, will you lead us?"

Matt nods and we all bow our heads. In his calm, gentle voice, Matt asks the Lord to mercifully guide our words and open our hearts. When we open our eyes, Grandma's head is still bowed. She sits perfectly still, staring at her hands.

"Well, we have a list here," Matt says, holding up our ream of notes.

Papa chuckles. "That's quite a stack of paper."

"Well, we had to do quite a bit of research since you and Sister Betty have refused to talk about anything that has happened in your family."

"I trust this research you've done isn't the idle gossip you've acquired from the Internet!" Grandma spits.

"The Internet is simply a communication tool," Matt says. "It's not gossip if the stories can be substantiated. Frankly, the people who shared their stories on the website were pretty brave, I think."

Papa leans back in his chair, crosses his arms over his chest, and guffaws. "Anyone can be brave when they're sitting behind a computer screen, writing anonymously."

But Matt doesn't hesitate. "Your granddaughter Rachel wrote an entire story using her full name. We're pretty sure we know the story now. We're here to give you a chance to be honest with us."

"What happens in my family is my business!" Papa snaps. "I'm under no obligation to answer questions from anyone!"

"We think you are obligated," Matt replies. "As the founder of The Assembly, you decide who is financially supported by your ministry. Your son David is a full-time pastor in The Assembly, and yet for years after his abusive behavior was reported, he was still not removed from leadership. We've talked with people who lived with David, and we're here today in hopes that you'll acknowledge the part you and Sister Betty played in covering up the domestic violence."

"Am I on trial here in my own home?" Papa bristles.

"No, we're simply here to tell you that unless you can be honest with us about what is going on, we can no longer be in The Assembly."

Papa reaches for his Bible and flips it open. In a stern voice he reads a passage about submitting to church leadership. Whipping his glasses off his nose, Papa glares at us. "I am not under your authority; you are under mine! You are not proceeding biblically! If you have a grievance with me, the Bible is clear that you are to entreat me with several witnesses!"

I reach for the stack of papers and hold it up. "These are our witnesses. We have spoken with all of them. All the stories are the same."

"Did you know about the abuse occurring in your son's family?" Matt asks.

Papa clutches the arms of his chair so hard his knuckles turn white. "I will not answer that!"

"Sister Betty, did you know about the abuse?" Matt asks.

"Don't you dare question my wife," Papa interrupts. "She has nothing to do with this!"

"So, you refuse to answer the questions?"

Papa stares at Matt, and when his eyes turn to me, I feel a sudden urge to relieve my bladder. "I need to use the restroom!" I squawk and struggle up from the couch. Nobody says a word. I hurry down the hall and into the bathroom. My heart is pounding with a mixture of elation and terror. *Papa isn't going to give in. We are nearing the end. Freedom is mere minutes away.*

I use the toilet and then wash my hands, looking at myself in the bathroom mirror. *This is the last time I'll ever use this bathroom. This is the last time I'll ever enter this house.* I touch my belly and smile. *This baby will be born into freedom.*

When I return to the living room, Papa is standing. He has his thumbs hitched in his belt loops, his chest puffed out. Matt is standing too. I pause at the edge of the room, suddenly wondering if this meeting will come to blows. Papa moves forward, jutting his face into Matt's.

"Woe to you!" he booms. "Woe to you! For with what measure you mete, it shall be measured to you!"

I glance at Grandma. Her face is as impassive as stone. She stares straight ahead, but in her lap, her hands twist a tissue to knots. I move toward the sofa and tap Matt on the shoulder. It is time to go.

"We'll pray for your repentance," Matt says.

"Leave my house!" Papa roars. "I will not forbear such disrespect!"

I grab my purse and back out of the room. With each step toward the door, I feel a chant rising in my heart. It is a growing drumbeat, a culmination of all these years: *Get out, get out, get out.* I reach for the door handle...

"Aren't you forgetting something?"

I turn, trembling. Papa stands at the entrance to the formal living room and points at Grandma, still seated. "Your grandmother would like to say good-bye."

I turn to Matt, my expression a silent question. He nods. We can do this one last thing. We can say good-bye.

Grandma rises from her chair as we reenter the room. I move toward her and look into her face. Grandma's ice-blue eyes are misty behind her glasses. A tear glints on her cheek. I open my arms and embrace her. Even though she has done nothing but make my life miserable, I don't want our last moment to be one of hostility. I embrace her because I can see a glint of her humanity—crushed as it is behind all that fear and evil behavior.

"Good-bye, Elizabeth," she says.

"Good-bye, Grandma," I answer. I give her one last look and walk toward Matt at the front door.

Papa stands by silently, jaw clenched so tight the muscles show on his cheeks. When I glance back, Papa George Geftakys is backlit by the window, and I can't see his face. He is simply a shadow.

We close the door quietly behind us.

Chapter 18

Do I Have to Like Oprah?

We changed our phone number, cut off all contact with everyone still involved in The Assembly, and moved to a different city. It was a sudden, difficult break, but it also felt strangely clean.

Our first purchase was a common household idol. Which is to say, we bought a television. The way I saw it, I had twenty-five years of TV watching to catch up on. We had quit the cult cold turkey. We were burned out physically, spiritually, and emotionally. Now all we wanted to do was relax and watch TV.

Even though I knew there would come a time when I'd have to process what had happened in The Assembly, I wasn't ready to deal with it. In the immediate aftermath of leaving, I was more concerned with figuring out how to work my remote control like a normal, mainstream American.

We'd been rocket launched out of our cloistered, closed-system religious world and into loud, secular, mainstream America. Adapting to life on the outside was thrilling and also completely disconcerting.

One of the first things I noticed after leaving The Assembly was how many hours there were in a day. Since infancy, I'd had my entire life arranged around meetings, outreaches, Bible studies, mission trips, and church-related activities. Overnight, that was all gone.

For the first time in my life—at age twenty-five—I was allowed to make my own schedule according to my own priorities. And so was Matt. Suddenly, he was picking up old hobbies: relandscaping the backyard, planning camping trips, and bodyboarding again.

But freedom was also strange. The unscheduled hours often felt like a cavernous vacuum. We didn't know how to live our lives without someone telling us what to do, where to go, when to arrive, and when to leave. What did normal people do with all their spare time? Then again, even my definition of spare time was wonky. I was, after all, a stay-at-home mom of three children aged three and under. My days, by American norms, were already very busy. I guess the fact that I *felt* that there were so many "extra hours" is proof of how insanely busy our lives had been inside The Assembly.

I'd never had a TV in my home and couldn't imagine wasting all that time just sitting around. On the other hand, I couldn't wait to gorge myself on all the sacrilegious entertainment.

Take Oprah. I didn't understand Oprah. I'd heard she was the most authentic woman on TV, but when I watched her show for the first time, I was disappointed. To me, she seemed like a fake personality, all heavy makeup and maudlin "aha moments." Even her ability to emote on cue seemed about as genuine as those prerecorded laugh tracks I heard on sitcoms. The only authentic thing I could see about Oprah was her megalomania.

Whenever I watched Oprah, I suspected she was manipulating me, requiring me to feel what she was feeling. It was like being in The Assembly, where Papa George required us to "rejoice!" on cue. After what I'd been through, I didn't want anyone—not even a famous personality—telling me how to feel.

Was it okay to not like Oprah? After leaving The Assembly, all I wanted was to be normal. As far as I could tell, everyone liked Oprah. Could I fit in without liking her?

Still, since I was home all day, I used TV as my shortcut to under-standing pop culture and assimilating into mainstream America. That made me prime bait for every putrid reality show, game show, cartoon, and newscast. I got emotionally involved in everything from *Barney and Friends* to *The Bachelor*. One night I went to bed crying because I couldn't believe Tony left Billie Jean at the altar on a trashy show called *Married by America*. "Why would he do that to her?" I wailed to Matt.

"The real question is, why are you watching that show?" he answered.

He had a point. To my chagrin, I had to admit my parents were right. TV was appalling drivel. But still I watched. I even watched commercials. This quickly became a problem.

Having grown up with very little exposure to TV advertising, I had no resistance to it. In The Assembly we took pride in our ignorance of what was cool and hip in The World. We were concerned with higher standards and "eternal values." But now, I wanted to know *everything* about what was hip and of-the-moment. Worst of all, I wanted to buy everything.

I began to feel that my life was meaningless without double-the-pleasure, double-the-fun spearmint gum. Or that newfangled front-loading washing machine. After watching a Diet Coke commercial that featured a carefree girl roller-skating at the beach, I developed a Diet Coke habit. I wanted to *be* that girl. I wanted that happy life hanging out with all my friends.

And there was the rub. As much as I was enjoying my unfettered access to television, I couldn't deny it was having a negative impact on my level of contentment. TV made me suddenly aware of all the things I *didn't* have: A fancy washer and dryer. A double-the-fun life. Friends to roller-skate with at the beach.

I'd left The Assembly feeling as if I now had everything I ever wanted: my freedom, my husband, and my children. But after just a few months of living in mainstream America and consuming too much TV, I felt as if I had nothing at all. TV had given me the impression that everyone else had loads of wonderful gadgets and tools and friends; networks of colleagues; and thriving, intact families.

"You know it's all just a show, right?" Matt asked me one evening while we sat on the front porch watching our little ones play in the yard. "It's all an illusion. Nobody has the glamorous life you see on TV."

"But it seems so real!" I said.

"You want it to be real. There's a big difference."

Was it all just a show? Did The World manage its image of hipness as carefully as The Assembly managed its image of holiness? Did The World pretend to have lots of friends just as The Assembly pretended to have lots of deeply spiritual relationships?

I'd told myself that leaving The Assembly was the solution we'd been waiting for, that freedom was all we needed to create our new-and-improved lives. I'd assumed that I could easily cobble together a patchwork quilt of belonging. If I drank Diet Coke, wore the right clothes, attended a thriving megachurch, and made friends with Southern Californian Christians, I'd find my place. I'd find my home.

Yes! This was my new plan for a better life!

But when I explain this to Matt, he seems unimpressed. "Why do we need a better life?" He gestures at our kids romping on the grass. "We have it all right here."

"Yes, yes, I know," I huff. "But what about pursuing our dreams, being successful, and building a new network for ourselves? What about getting involved in a new church? I hear Calvary Chapel has a great kids' program and even a school!"

Matt glances at me, eyebrow raised. "What about being content with what we already have?"

This gives me pause. Is this life good enough for me?

Maybe it is good enough for Matt. But then again, it doesn't take much to make him happy. I am the one who wants more. I am the one who feels The Assembly held me back, denied my full potential. I want all life has to offer.

I want to *carpe diem*. I want to *carpe all* the *diems*.

"You need to relax," Matt says as I pace the porch. "The End of the World isn't happening tonight, so sit down and watch your babies. Hold 'em while you can."

His phrasing stops me cold. It isn't the End of the World? Yes, I know that. But I am acting as if all will be lost if I don't reinvent myself immediately.

Is it possible that even though I've left The Assembly, that frantic way of living hasn't left me? Have I simply transferred my apocalypse mentality into a new context? The thought haunts and enrages me. All I want is to freely pursue the life I'd been dreaming about forever. What is so wrong with that?

I look at Matt, contentedly watching our kids play. Even during the worst of our times in The Assembly, he'd remained unflappable and calm. I admire his serenity and his ability to weather the storms of life. But I also find myself feeling resentful.

I blow out my cheeks in frustration. We are out of The Assembly, but we are still at odds with each other. I'm beginning to think maybe I want to have a career. Maybe I want to go back to school. Matt seems content with what we already have: taking the occasional camping trip, puttering around the house tackling DIY projects. Do we even want the same things out of life?

I spin on my heels and go inside, leaving Matt alone on the porch to watch our children play in the gloaming.

"So, do you live around here?" I ask a mom at the playground as we push our little ones on the baby swings. Despite my casual demeanor I've been feverishly racking my brain for a pleasantly nonchalant question.

"Oh, just a few months," she answers breezily.

"We've only been here three weeks. Do you like it?"

She nods and pauses to wipe a smudge of dirt from her little boy's cheek. "Yeah, it's nice. We moved here for my husband's job."

"Oh! We did too!" I chirp.

It isn't entirely untrue. Part of the reason we moved from Fullerton to a home in Tustin was to be closer to Matt's job. But mostly, we moved to start over fresh, to rebuild our lives from scratch. I desperately want to make friends but am terribly unsure about how to do that. How do normal people go about it? I don't know how to engage people without trying to convert them to Christ. I don't know how to have a conversation without steering it toward Questions of Eternal Significance.

"Parker!" the mom yells suddenly. "Sit on your bottom to go down the slide!" She glances at me and shrugs a little. "That boy would fly down the slide face first if I let him."

I burst into laughter. "Yeah, I know how that goes! My oldest boy has no fear."

She chuckles and we continue pushing our tots in the swings. I sneak a glance at her face, trying to read her. She seems preoccupied, pushing her baby with one hand and watching her son on the slide. Did I laugh too loudly? Do I seem too pushy? What else can I talk about to build a connection with her?

In the toddler swing, Jude has started to fuss. I slow the swing and hand him a little teething toy to gnaw on. "You've got a new tooth coming in, don'tcha, big boy?" I say loud enough for the other mom to hear.

She glances over. I meet her eye and smile. "He's been quite a little fusser these past few days!"

She nods. "My Bella here got her first molar last week."

"Ouch!"

"Yeah, no joke. Poor baby girl, it's been a rough few days for us."

"Us too!"

We're talking! We're connecting!

"Is she your youngest?" I ask, trying to keep my tone even and steady, masking my eagerness.

"Yes. She's nine months old, and then I have Parker over there; he's four."

"This is Jude. He's eight months old! Our babies are only one month apart! They should be friends!" As soon as I say it, I feel ridiculous. I sound desperate and needy. Wait. I *am* desperate and needy.

"Sure, let's exchange numbers. I'm Sheryl, by the way."

"Hi, Sheryl! I'm Elizabeth! I'd love to hang out again sometime soon!"

"Sure thing," says Sheryl.

I can scarcely contain my delight. Sure-Thing Sheryl and I, we are going to be friends. Jude is fussing again, so I haul him out of the baby swing and bounce him on my hip.

"Mom! Watch me!" It is my son James, about to brave the monkey bars. I glance back at Sheryl. She is busy wiping Bella's nose. If I walk away without confirming the day we'll meet up, will she remember to call me?

"Mom! Watch!"

"Sheryl, it was wonderful to meet you," I say. "Let's talk soon?"

She doesn't look up. "Sure thing," she repeats.

I force myself to walk away. Is it really a sure thing? Does it mean I should call today or wait a few days? Does it mean she will call first?

This is another frustrating aspect of assimilation. The way normal people talk in mainstream America often flummoxes me. I've been taught to speak frankly and with righteous moral clarity. When I say the word *literally,* I actually mean "literally."

When I was growing up in fundamentalism, yes was yes and no was no—at least when it came to stating our beliefs. But in mainstream America, opinions and beliefs are stated in a deliberately open-ended manner. People say "sort of" and "kind of" and end their declarative statements with question marks. Apparently, specificity of language has gone extinct.

Which is to say, just because Sheryl told me "sure thing" we'd meet up again, I'm not sure if she meant this literally or figuratively or maybe or sort of. This new life in mainstream America is sorta, kinda, like, baffling.

A few days later I call Sheryl. She doesn't answer, so I leave a message in my best imitation of a breezy, noncommittal, question-marks-in-random-places, mainstream American voice—except my fundamentalist voice keeps trying to take over, and eventually, the message becomes a train wreck: "Hi, Sheryl! It's Elizabeth, the mom from the park whose baby boy is one month younger than your daughter? Call me back if you want but it's okay if you can't but I'll be available between the hours of seven and eight thirty to discuss a best-friend play date for our kids and we can be best friends too! Or we can be casual friends. If you want. Maybe. Sort of. Please call me!"

I hang up in tears.

Sure-Thing Sheryl never calls back.

I don't blame her. She probably has good, healthy boundaries and could smell my neediness a mile away.

Independent Distributor for Jesus

This is a first: people are trying to convert *me*.

A few months after we left The Assembly, a woman notices me admiring a set of handwoven oven mitts in the aisle of a home-goods store. She strikes up a conversation, and I fall for her friendliness. "I'd love to hang out sometime," she says and hands me her business card. I am thrilled.

She calls me a few days later. "I'm in a bit of a hurry," she begins apologetically. "But I could sense how eager you were in the store, so I wanted to make sure I got you on my calendar right away!"

I'm confused. "What calendar?"

"For a home party! I just know you're gonna love these kitchen gadgets!"

"What kitchen gadgets?"

There is an awkward pause. "I gave you my card, right?"

"Right, yes. I remember." What am I missing? I remember glancing at her card but haven't made the connection between her name and the title beneath it: *Independent Distributor*.

"Don't worry, my home parties are always lots of fun!"

I recognize something in her tone—that same, extracheerful sales-pitchy voice my dad used when attempting to convince a reluctant unbeliever that a personal relationship with Jesus Christ was always lots of fun.

"Wait, were you pretending to be my friend?" I blurt into the phone.

"What?"

"Were you just being nice to me in the store so I'd let you sell your stuff to my friends at a home party?" (I wasn't about to tell her that I don't have any friends.)

"Oh, I genuinely *like* you!" she exclaims. "And I hope we can become friends!"

"But first I need to schedule a home party?"

"Well, sure. Wouldn't that be fun?"

"Um, no. Not really."

"I'm surprised to hear that, Elizabeth," she chides. "You seemed so interested in our conversation at the store."

"I was interested in *you*."

"Well, thank you! And I'm interested in *you*!"

"Um, okay..."

"So, if you're not interested in hosting a home party, would you mind returning those promotional items I gave you?"

"You mean the 'free samples'?"

"Well, they were only free if you were going to host a party—"

"I need to go now," I say and hang up.

It is suddenly dawning on me that I'd done the exact same thing to people: pretended to be their friend in order to get them to buy something. Instead of selling kitchen gadgets, I'd been a multilevel marketer for The Assembly.

I'd been an Independent Distributor of Salvation.

How can I resent this woman for trying to sell me Tupperware? I'd done worse. I'd sold Jesus.

Everyone was selling Jesus. At least, that's how it seemed to me when we started attending an evangelical megachurch in Southern California.

We'd tried taking a break from church, but not going at all was actually *more* uncomfortable. For better or worse, going to church on Sundays was ingrained in our DNA.

For us, coming from The Assembly where meetings were starkly simple, going to a megachurch was dazzling: we saw vending machines, coffee shops, bookstores, gymnasiums, and free childcare. When we arrived, we received little buzzers to keep track of each of our children in Sunday school, and when we left, there were parking attendants directing all the traffic.

After sitting through three-hour meetings in The Assembly, our kids loved attending Fun Megachurch.

"Look! Crafts!" Jewel chortled. She proudly showed off a gluey mess of bedazzled crosses covered in an avalanche of glitter.

"I pwayed wif Wegos!" James reported, all wide eyed and astonished.

Even Jude was doted on in baby Sunday school, coddled on the laps of sweet grandmothers and serenaded with *Wee Sing Bible Songs*.

And the adults got four-star service too. There were small groups for every imaginable demographic: kids, preteens, teens, college-age adults, singles, married couples with young children, empty nesters, and bikers. There were moms' groups, support groups, and a divorced ladies' Bible study. There were cruises—er, "spiritual pilgrimages"—you could take with the pastor and his wife to see the Holy Land. Joining a megachurch was sort of like becoming a member of a country club except better because all your dues/tithes were tax deductible.

People referred to the church grounds as a "campus"—and it really felt that big. It was loud, crowded, and overflowing with an array of worship options. Did we want to sit inside or outside? Did we want to watch the service on the jumbo screen in the gymnasium or listen through loudspeakers on the patio? Perhaps we were hungry and needed breakfast in the church coffee shop first?

Everyone was cheerful and friendly and casual. I couldn't believe this was *church*. Where was all the suffering and bearing of crosses? Church felt like Disneyland, the Happiest Cross on Earth.

Months passed, then a year. During that time, we got updates from friends still inside about continuing chaos in The Assembly. Several women had come forward with allegations that Papa George had had affairs with them. My parents had stepped down from leadership. Most of the sister churches were disbanding. Through it all, Matt and I made a conscious choice not to involve ourselves in the ensuing fallout.

For the most part, we were just too exhausted. We'd done our part: we confronted Papa George and Grandma Betty about Uncle David's abuse. Any further allegations simply confirmed what we'd already suspected, and I, for one, didn't have the energy to hash it all out. We'd shared our findings with those who would listen and quit the cult cold turkey.

I had barely talked to Mom or Dad. What was there to say? Initially, Mom had said she understood why we decided to leave, but Dad still couldn't believe we were "forsaking" the one true church. And we couldn't believe they were staying in a corrupt one. Every time we tried to talk, the conversation devolved into a hurtful argument. It was safer to go silent.

I still wanted my kids to have a relationship with their grandparents, but I also needed the space to figure out what that would look like. It was becoming clear to me that my social blunders in mainstream America were indicators I'd never learned proper personal boundaries. I was beginning to suspect there were other problems too.

One day in church my past caught up with me. I was blindsided by a panic attack right in the middle of a Fun Megachurch service.

We are sitting in our usual pew when a strange, nauseous feeling hits me. My heart speeds up, and my hands start shaking. A muffled roar fills my ears, and my vision caves in. I grip Matt's leg and then, afraid I will vomit, stumble up the aisle and into the church lobby.

"Are you okay?" asks an usher. I can only stare. I don't know what is happening.

Two men shepherd me into a metal folding chair, and another hands me a paper cup of water.

Matt hurries into the lobby, but I still can't speak. My throat has closed completely. I lean over my legs, hanging my head between my knees, and try to breathe slowly. Above me, I can hear the men discussing the situation in whispers. Matt says something about my being exhausted, and the ushers note that I will need to be moved soon in order to make way for the exiting congregation.

"Scared!" It is my voice speaking. A blurting, frantic voice that sounds like a wounded animal.

One of the ushers glances at me. "What?"

"I'm scared!" I repeat.

"What are you scared of?"

I shake my head. I don't know.

"Maybe she was feeling claustrophobic," Matt offers. "We probably need to sit near the aisle from here on out."

I can only nod. *Sure. Claustrophobia. That's it.*

So we started arriving late to church so we could sit on the aisle instead of being asked to move into the center of the pew. We located ourselves near exits. We left early.

But the second time a panic attack hit me, a seed of doubt sprouted in my mind: Was something wrong with me? Why couldn't I stay calm in church? I was mortified by my own lack of self-control. To make matters worse, I was on campus every day because Jewel was there for kindergarten. There was no escape. My brain was on high alert all the time.

As my anxiety progressed, the panic attacks were followed by recurring nightmares about The Assembly. And then I started experiencing flashbacks during sermons. Sometimes a sermon topic would remind me of something from The Assembly, and I'd either go limp, staring blankly at the pew in front of me, or else run out in a blind panic.

Within a few months I was unable to get through a church service without bolting up the aisle. I started running out the door, across the campus, and to the parking lot—much to the consternation of the ushers who scrambled to quietly open and shut doors as I rushed past.

I would crumple into the car and weep. Why was this happening? I had believed that leaving The Assembly was enough. I thought I'd be able to start over fresh in a new church. Why couldn't I just get over my past?

At the time, I didn't have the words to describe what had happened to me inside The Assembly. I knew I had suffered, but I wasn't about to call myself an abuse victim—that seemed so weak. I saw myself as a survivor and fully believed I could adapt to the outside world without any help. Therapy, I believed, was for people with weak faith.

But I couldn't deny that my body was reacting as if it had a mind of its own. It collapsed and hyperventilated without my permission. I sweated profusely, my stomach clenched with nausea, and my skin broke out in psoriasis. Something beyond my control was happening.

Soon anxiety was leaking into every corner of my life, washing over me at random moments. It was affecting my ability to function. Once, while driving on the freeway, I had to pull over before ascending an overpass because I had the sudden fear that the wheel would swerve out of my hands and send my car flying off the edge.

Matt saw my increasing anxiety, but he didn't know how to help. Both of us had been firmly indoctrinated with the idea that therapy was not for Christians. One Sunday after I fled the service during a "prophecy update," he was fed up. Suddenly, it was as if Assembly Matt was back. I sobbed in the car on the way home while he told me I was ruining church for our children. Didn't I want them to have a positive experience? Couldn't I just soldier through for the children's sake?

"I'm sorry, I'm sorry, I'm sorry," I said.

And I tried to soldier. Until the next panic attack hit, and the next and the next.

One morning, I freak out in our favorite local coffee shop, The Lost Bean, and it isn't anywhere near church. We had just placed our drink orders when I am distracted by the headlines on a newspaper lying on a nearby table. I pause to flip through the pages. When I look up, Matt is gone.

It is immediate, the panic. My whole body starts shaking. I dash out of the shop and stand in the brilliant morning sunshine, trembling. My thoughts tumble over themselves, and my heart races. *The Rapture has happened, and I've been Left Behind.*

Part of me knows this is ridiculous and irrational. But that doesn't stop my body from behaving as if I am eight again, crying on the floor of my parents' kitchen, convinced the world has ended.

When Matt finally emerges from the coffee shop—he'd simply gone to the restroom—he sees my white face and trembling hands. He folds me into his arms and holds me until I stop shaking.

That night as we lie in bed, Matt strokes my hair and speaks softly. "I don't know what else to do. Do you think we can get some help? Find a therapist to help you?"

I nod. I've already e-mailed an ex-Assembly member, explained my symptoms, and asked if she knows of a therapist in our area. It is time.

I can see that although I've left one high-demand religious environ-ment, I have simply entered a new one. By plunging into another church before giving myself time to heal from what happened in The Assembly, I am simply repeating the cycle.

I've survived a dysfunctional, apocalyptic childhood. But I am still living in a murderous whirlwind of anxiety.

I have left fundamentalism, but fundamentalism hasn't left me.

Chapter 20

Religious PTSD

"How did you cope with all those spankings?" my therapist asks.

I twist the tissue between my fingers and take a deep breath. I'm not sure how to describe what happened to me during a spanking. I look up at Rae. She is tall and willowy, and she wears her platinum-white hair cropped feisty short. She is probably in her midsixties. I like her artistic, dangly earrings.

"You're safe here," Rae says, as if reading my mind.

I've been coming to see her for about three months, and it has taken me all this time to start talking about my daily childhood spankings. I finally blurt it out: "I just disappeared into the bedspread patterns."

Rae nods as if this makes perfect sense and jots something on her notepad.

"Is that weird?" I ask. "I know it sounds…"

"It doesn't sound crazy at all, Elizabeth. Can you explain what 'disappearing into the bedspread' was like for you?"

"Well, Mom always made me stretch out on the bed with my bottom exposed. Just before she started spanking me, I would focus on a tiny flower in the bedspread and send my mind into it. Sorta send my mind far away from what was happening."

"Ah," Rae comments. "We call that 'disassociation.'"

Disassociation. It is a word I have heard before but never in reference to that mind trick I had used to cope. That trick isn't a figment of my imagination. It was real. It had a *name*. And if the coping mechanism was real, it means what I have experienced was real too.

I shoot a horrified look at my therapist. "But…but I don't want it to sound like I was abused or anything. My parents loved me! I don't want to dishonor them!"

"Elizabeth, we honor our parents by telling the truth."

"I feel like I'm betraying them. I still love them, and in many ways, they really were good parents. I mean, they did give me this belief that God exists, a belief I can't seem to shake—even if I don't read my Bible anymore."

Rae nods. "Perhaps God wants to reveal Himself to you in other ways. First, you need to feel safe. Your brain needs to feel safe before it can start healing itself. Right now, your brain is still on guard. It perceives threats. Reading the Bible and attending church are anxiety triggers for you."

Triggers. This is another word Rae often uses. Before coming to Rae, I simply had no compass for navigating my mental well-being. In The Assembly, emotional states like depression and anxiety were viewed as moral failures. Sins. My range of emotion was categorized into two spiritual feelings: rejoicing or not rejoicing. So when our doomsday theology made me feel anxious, I believed those negative feelings were the result of "being in sin" and that I could just "pray them away." I could pray my way into rejoicing.

But now I am learning how to feel all my feelings and express them appropriately. I am learning it is okay to feel sad when something sad happens. It is acceptable to feel angry when I realize I was treated cruelly. Everything in The Assembly was about control, control, control. Rae, on the other hand, is trying to teach me to let go, let go, let go.

"Instead of disassociating and numbing out, can you practice being present?" she asks.

"I don't know what 'being present' means," I say. "It sounds hokey."

"It means to stop and just breathe for a moment. Ask yourself if you're hungry, angry, lonely, or tired. Once you've identified what you're feeling, then ask yourself, what do I need to do to take care of myself in this present moment?"

"That sounds too easy," I say.

"Well, for someone who is accustomed to working really hard to win God's approval, I can understand why it sounds too easy. Just try it this week, and you can tell me how it goes, okay?"

I went home that day and started practicing being present. Each time I felt anxiety starting to rattle my body, I took slow, deep breaths and noticed things in my immediate environment. One day at a time I started building a habit of being present. I stopped watching the news. Instead, I began to interact with reality. I planted flowers, took my dog for walks, and read aloud with my children.

I stopped listening to the frantic voices of talk radio. Instead, I covered empty coffee cans with pretty fabric and filled them with sharpened pencils for my kids' teachers. I snapped pictures of flowers growing in an abandoned lot. I accepted a neighbor's invitation to attend her Bunco group. I began journaling again.

It was a strange paradox that simple, ordinary changes, like reengaging my life and proceeding slowly and mindfully, could have such a beneficial impact on my brain. But it was happening. It was real. Maybe recovery didn't have to be complicated. It didn't have to be fraught.

The gentler I was with myself, the safer I felt. The safer I felt, the less anxiety I experienced. My attacks slowly lessened, first in intensity and then in frequency.

Still, taking it easy was...hard. It was difficult to believe that building a new life for myself outside The Assembly didn't require the same kind of stringent rigor with which I'd been raised. Whenever she caught me being too hard on myself or making things more difficult than they needed to be, my therapist reminded me that healing was just a breath away.

Eventually I felt safe and brave enough to stop attending a church that triggered my anxiety. As soon as Jewel finished kindergarten, we quietly left Fun Megachurch.

Two years passed. My Bible was disappearing under a veil of neglect. One day as I ran my dust rag across its cover, my grandfather's words echoed in my mind. *"This book will keep you from sin, or sin will keep you from this book."*

Was sin keeping me from this book?

I shook out my dust rag and continued cleaning my room, swallowing the guilty lump that had formed in my throat. Ever since leaving The Assembly, I couldn't read my Bible without breaking into a cold sweat. Every time I opened it, I heard my grandfather's voice, his inflection and interpretation. Papa George's voice so fully saturated every passage that I could not, as I'd heard evangelicals say, "read the Bible for myself."

Not reading my Bible meant I was backsliding. I had been taught from infancy that if I didn't read my Bible, I wouldn't know God. In The Assembly I couldn't imagine having a relationship with God apart from daily Scripture reading.

From childhood, I interpreted every scintilla of my human experience through a "biblical worldview." I didn't know how to make decisions without first consulting the Bible. Everything we did was guided by a process Papa George called "claiming promises." When faced with choosing classes for college, I was expected to pray over my schedule and then "claim a promise" to help me decide between, say, Political Science or Psychology 101.

My parents had taught me that God cared about the tiniest decision, and the only way I could know God's will for my life was through daily Bible reading. It was the fundamentalist equivalent of learning to see, as William Blake once wrote, "a world in a grain of sand."

The problem, of course, was that we believed God was confined to our particular grain of sand.

And furthermore, now that I was out of The Assembly, I could see how we'd used the Bible as our own personal crystal ball. The process of "claiming promises" had often resulted in disastrous decisions. I'd seen entire families uproot and move to a different part of the country without so much as a job prospect or place to live because they'd "claimed a promise."

One family had moved because they'd "claimed a promise" in the book of Psalms that mentioned a place called "Salem." That took them to Salem, Oregon. They spent a year floundering around the Pacific Northwest, trying to find work and plant a new Assembly, eventually returning to California broke and unemployed. What was the difference, I wondered, between God speaking and humans just making stuff up?

I was discovering that real life in the real world just didn't work on magical formulas like "claiming promises." At least, not without giving me anxiety attacks. And yet, I didn't know how to read my Bible any other way.

I stood in my bedroom that day and wondered if my faith was doomed. If God could be found only in the pages of my Bible and reading my Bible gave me anxiety, how could I continue my journey of faith? Well, I hadn't been reading my Bible anyway, and God hadn't struck me with lightning yet, so...

I grab my Bible and walk to the living room. My bookcases are overflowing. Back when Matt wanted to become a full-time pastor in The

Assembly, he'd collected concordances, Hebrew-Greek lexicons, biblical histories, and commentaries. Our shelves are loaded with Christian writers my grandfather admired, and I have some of them displayed between the globe bookends Papa George gave me when I was a child. I decide to hide my Bible behind E. H. Broadbent's *The Pilgrim Church*.

And then I step back. All these men. All their talking and writing and preaching and arguing over Scripture interpretation, all of them sitting on my shelf making me break out in hives. T. Austin-Sparks, G. Campbell Morgan, Watchman Nee, George Whitefield, James Strong and his totally exhausting Bible concordance, Samuel Rutherford and his letters, Jonathan Edwards and his huge freak-outs about falling into the hands of an angry God. And then there was my grandfather, George Geftakys, with his own self-published book, *Testimony to Jesus*.

Well, these men can just sit here on my shelf and argue with each other. I am done listening to their voices in my head. If I am going to find my way back to God, I will start from scratch. I will choose the way of the illiterate. I mean, if God is abounding in mercy and loving-kindness, then surely there is a way to God reserved especially for those who cannot read!

I want *that* way.

I am fed up with reading about God through the male perspective only. I want to experience the God who inspired me as a child, the God who found me long before I could comprehend a single word in my Bible.

I want to experience God pursuing *me* for once. I am tired of seeking, striving, and knock-knock-knocking on heaven's door. I no longer want to know that silent, capricious, harsh God who would just as soon throw me into the fires of hell as save me. I am challenging God to pursue me like someone who has never been exposed to the Bible.

Love me, God. I dare You.

Andrew was grizzled, gouty, and wreck kneed. But every day for an entire school year, he greeted me with unflagging cheer as I crossed the street to drop off and pick up my kids from school.

"Hey, Elizabeth!" Andrew would roar as I approached the crosswalk. "It might be cloudy this morning, but that don't mean the sun ain't shinin'!"

I'd never met a crossing guard who took such joy in his job. His boundless enthusiasm, genuine interest in others, and mastery of fifteen-second conversations never ceased to surprise me. He could bust out anecdotes, jokes, and philosophical reflections faster than any polished preacher I'd ever heard. But unlike the preachers, Andrew was unpretentious.

"Really missing my kids this year," he told me one morning near Thanksgiving. "I've made so many mistakes in my life, and they don't wanna see me no more."

"I'm sorry to hear that," I said, thinking guiltily about my own parents.

"Hey, I might got big problems, but at least I got confession too. God's gotta forgive me!" And he burst into his guffaw, hoisting high his STOP sign as he ba-ha-ha'd his way across the street.

I chuckled at this ruined man, gimping his way back and forth every day. He was poor, a sober alcoholic, and a brokenhearted father struggling to maintain a connection with his grown children. But despite it all, he had joy to give away.

"Gotta ride my bike to Mass today," Andrew announced one morning. "Stickin' close to God keeps me humble, keeps me sane. That priest there, that Father Al? Man oh man, he don't mess 'round." Andrew mimicked a sword piercing his heart. "Gah! He gets me ever' time!"

I nodded as if I understood, but I didn't. I didn't know anything about priests or Catholicism except what I'd learned in fundamentalism: that the Catholic Church was the Whore of Babylon. Also, Catholics worshiped Mary. But for Andrew's sake, I pretended it was cool. Besides, I had bigger things to worry about.

I was pregnant again. With twins. It had been a wonderful surprise—but a surprise nonetheless. I never weathered my first trimesters very well, and even Andrew the crossing guard noticed me dragging each day.

"Lotta times I see you, looks like you're haulin' the world around on your shoulders," he commented. "So I got this for you." He pressed a small booklet of prayers into my hand and smiled his gap-toothed smile.

"Oh, um. Okay," I fumbled.

"I know you're pregnant, so try the Memorare," Andrew suggested. "Mary knows all about suffering for the sake of her child."

"Okay, thanks," I said—not having any idea what the Memorare might be. Still, if a beat-up old crossing guard managed to stay joyful by saying those prayers, I figured I could at least try it.

That night I open the Memorare and am immediately disappointed. It is a prayer asking for Mary's intercession. *No way. I'm not praying to Mary!*

I want *direct* access to God. I don't want to have to go through some middle man. Or middle woman. I'm not about to ask for help from another *woman*. Who is Mary, anyway? She is just Jesus's mother.

Frustrated, I slap closed the prayer booklet and stalk toward the kitchen to throw it away. As I pass my bookcases filled with Bible commentaries, I pause. Here are all these great men of God, weighing down my shelves with their words. Haven't they taken up enough space in my life, in my head, and in my heart? Smiling, I slip the prayer booklet between the weighty tomes. Maybe Mary has something important to add to the conversation. After all, it is about *her* Son.

Then I realize: She isn't *just* Jesus's mother. She is the mother of our Lord and Savior. Mary is important.

I touch my tender belly and think of the twins growing inside me. I'm not just a mother either. I am important.

The thought breaks over me like the rising dawn of a new day: *What if God is pursuing me through the gentle love of His Son's mother? What if, knowing that all masculine roads to God are blocked for me, Jesus has sent His mother to lead me back to Him?*

I turn away from the bookcase, a sliver of apprehension running up my spine. These are dangerous thoughts. God uses *men* to accomplish His plan of salvation. I know this. I've been taught this.

But as I pass the bookcase each day—not reading, not praying, still living an intentionally illiterate spiritual life—I can't help but wonder if by ignoring Mary I am missing something important.

Chapter 21

If You Can't Find Jesus, Look for His Mother

The intensive-care nurses can't find a vein. My underweight, premature daughter screams as they prod and prick her tiny arms with a needle.

"Please, let me hold her," I beg, clutching my freshly sutured stomach. The gash of my C-section feels like hot barbed wire wrapped around my middle. I sway slightly and place a steadying hand on my baby's incubator.

One of the nurses glances at me. "We can't let you hold her right now."

"Touch her?" I whisper.

The other nurse shakes her head and gestures for me to take a seat in a nearby chair. It has been seventeen hours since I was rushed to the hospital. Every fiber in my being aches to hold my babies—but all I can do is stand by and watch.

"We may have to go for a vein in her head," one of the nurses says.

I think I might faint. A vein in my baby's *head*? I'm not sure I can watch them prod Jasiel's tiny cranium.

Unable to stay with me in the hospital due to pressing needs at work, Matt left earlier that morning. "Please don't go," I'd begged.

"Elizabeth, we didn't plan for the babies to be born this early. I'm sorry, but I wasn't prepared. I have to go finish some things."

It makes sense, of course. Always dutiful, Matt wasn't about to leave his boss in the lurch. But I felt and still feel abandoned. And completely overwhelmed. Within a few hours we've gone from being a manageable family of five to a family of seven—with twins in the neonatal intensive-care unit of the hospital.

I stand up from the chair and walk over to my daughter's incubator. I watch her suffer. The helplessness is so overwhelming I'm afraid I might vomit. I brace myself against the incubator and silently cry out for help. *O God, help me. Help my baby.*

Almost immediately, I feel something shift. The slightest easing of pain, a gentle salve of grace. *This is a small taste of what Mary felt while watching her Son suffer.*

I take a deep breath. I've never once felt a kinship with Mary. All the heroes of my fundamentalist upbringing were men. We loved and exalted the apostle Paul or John the Revelator. We quoted Romans or pondered the Epistles, but I never heard a sermon devoted exclusively to Mary. We studied our Bibles backward and forward but somehow had entirely neglected to meditate on Mary's hymn of praise to God as recorded in Luke 1:46–55.

I begin to wonder if I've never felt close to Mary because I've been trained to look elsewhere. I blindly adopted the male-dominated narrative I learned in fundamentalism. Now it seems this neglect of Mary in both doctrine and devotion has cut me off from the maternal comfort I need.

Which hero of my faith can comfort me as my body leaks postbirth blood and my breasts swell with nourishing milk? Even all the beautiful psalms of King David can't touch the depth of this, my female human experience. I am woman. I am mother. Where is *my* mediator, the one who is intimately acquainted with *my* sorrows?

I need a woman's touch, a woman's understanding, a woman's empathy to comfort me as I watch my babies suffer in the hospital. I wrap my arms around my birth-sore body and gaze at the incubators, the two precious babies fighting for survival beneath the cords and wires, beeping monitors and pricking needles. A crack of light appears in my consciousness.

Mary understands. Mary watched her child suffer, and there was nothing she could do about it. Mary understands.

I smile, remembering a bumper sticker I'd seen and how offensive it seemed to me at the time. *Those ridiculous Catholics,* I'd thought. *Always diminishing the centrality of Christ.* But now, that bumper sticker means something to me: "If you can't find Jesus, look for His mother."

Now I need her. "Pray for me," I whisper, gazing at my tiny offspring. "Pray for us." The tension in my heart eases a little more. I pray again. I don't know all the right words. But I ask for her intercession.

Warmth like the softest baby blanket falls gently over my shoulders. I feel the quiet assurance that no matter what happens, all will be well. I glance up. Nothing in the hospital room has changed. The babies still scream. The monitors still beep. The nurses are still struggling to find a vein in my daughter's body. And yet I suddenly know I'm not alone. All will be well. Both of my twin baby girls will be okay.

Jesus has sent His mother to comfort me.

I'm going to the Catholic church because I don't know where else to find a way to God that feels safe. Maybe the Mother of God can lead me back...

Several months have passed since the mysterious maternal serenity I experienced in the hospital while standing over my twins. That moment with Mary was the first time I'd felt a kind of spiritual safety. And I want more of it.

I've been inside a Catholic church only a handful of times, mostly as a tourist. Once I attended Mass. So the first time I drive to my local parish I am nervous. I creep in all jittery and furtive, glancing over my shoulder before sliding into a back pew. As fundamentalists, we didn't have symbols, statues, crosses, or stained-glass windows. It takes me a few moments to adjust to the lingering scent of incense, the perfume of fresh flowers at the altar, and the profound hush that seems to permeate the air I breathe.

I crouch in the pew, working up courage to look at the massive crucifix behind the altar. Finally, I raise my eyes. I feel shock. The crucifix is so garish. Why does it have to be so bloody and brutal? Would it kill them to clean Jesus up a bit, make His death a little more presentable?

Protestant churches we've attended since leaving The Assembly featured tidy, empty crosses, duly sanitized for comfortable viewing. Even in Sunday school my kids used crayons, glitter, and sticker hearts to decorate chubby little cartoon crosses. Cute crosses.

This crucifix—it practically glories in its shame.

I glance around the rest of the church, my eyes settling on a statue of Jesus with a—what is it? A thorn-crowned heart poking out of His sternum? I think I might gag. Where is the nuance? Apparently, Catholics don't appreciate subtlety.

I let myself relax into the pew and gaze at the crucifix. If nothing else, I have to appreciate its stark honesty. Something is real here. The crucifix addresses death and suffering head-on. The crucifix isn't exactly "seeker friendly"; staring at it, I am forced to acknowledge the brutality of Jesus's death. The sheer obviousness of it is embarrassing, really. But it is also earnest.

I stay for only ten minutes.

As I pull away in my car, I realize this was the first time I'd been inside a church and felt peaceful.

I began to make a quiet habit of visiting St. Cecilia's whenever I had a spare moment. I attended Mass on weekday mornings, hauling my twins with me—one on each hip. I popped in for quick prayers while running errands. To my surprise, the rituals of Mass were not monotonous but calming. The Rosary was not "vain repetition" but deeply meditative.

One warm May afternoon while out running errands, I decide to stop by the church for a quick prayer. I pull into the parking lot and am surprised to see it full. It isn't the usual time for Mass, and I am confused. Is there some sort of service going on I don't know about? I duck into the church, determined to say my prayers anyway.

I gradually realize this is some kind of special service honoring "the Virgin," and it includes crowning Mary's statue with flowers. I feel annoyed. *Oh, Catholics. Do they always have to make such a big deal out of her?*

But then I catch myself. Isn't this why I have been coming to the Catholic church—to find Mary? Am I not hoping she can somehow lead me back to Jesus?

Yes, but I'm not ready for this—the placing of flowers on a statue, a blatant display of singing songs to the "Mother of God"! I duck back out of the church and stomp angrily across the parking lot. All glory belongs to God alone. To grant honor elsewhere is idolatry. Isn't it?

Halfway to my car I feel a piercing blow to my conscience. It stops me short. I suddenly understand that by storming out of the church in a huff, I'm behaving disrespectfully toward Jesus's mother. And...um... Jesus isn't superhappy about that.

I quickly wheel myself around and scamper back into church. I scoot into a row and respectfully wait out the rest of the service. When it is over, I make my way to the statue of Mary. I kneel. "I'm sorry," I whisper. And then: *This is ridiculous. I'm apologizing to a statue!*

I check myself again. I remind myself that I need a new way. All the old ways back to God are blocked for me. In the hospital, Mary was a lifeline, pulling my frightened soul to safety.

I fumble through my purse and find the old battered prayer book that Andrew the crossing guard gave me over a year ago. I find the Memorare. After all, I've come to the church today because I am desperate. Humbled, I say the prayer.

> Remember, O most gracious Virgin Mary, that never was it
> known that anyone who fled to your protection, implored your
> help, or sought your intercession was left unaided. Inspired with
> this confidence, I fly unto you, O Virgin of virgins, my Mother;
> to you I come, before you I stand, sinful and sorrowful. O Mother
> of the Word Incarnate, despise not my petitions, but in your
> mercy hear and answer me. Amen.

I don't know how this prayer will be answered. But when I leave the church, I know she heard me. It is enough.

The next morning, Matt is incredulous.

"After everything we went through in The Assembly, why would you want to go to a church that regularly makes headlines with scandals by men in authority?" he asks. "The Catholic Church is the biggest cult of them all!"

"Well, every church has its problems."

"That's an understatement."

"I can't explain it, Matt. I just feel safe there. I have this connection with Mary that's helping me understand Jesus again."

Matt rolls over in bed and looks at me. "I just think you're infatuated with how different it is. All the stained glass, candles, incense, the sense of antiquity. I get it. Ritual is calming."

"So you're saying I only like the Catholic Church because of my *feelings*?"

Matt shrugs. "Am I missing something?"

"Well, Jesus is there. Literally. Catholics believe the Eucharist is the literal body and blood of Jesus."

"Do you believe that, Elizabeth?"

"I think it's a possibility."

"That's crazy!"

"I know. Then again, the claims of Jesus are pretty crazy too."

"But what else? What else is drawing you there? Why are you always looking for something better?"

"I'm not looking for something better, Matt. I just want something *real*. If Jesus really *is* present in the Eucharist, I want to be as close to that as possible. And...there's something else too."

"What?"

"I'm also drawn to Catholicism because Catholics *embrace* mystery. They have this deep reverence for the mysteries of life and the ways of God. There's room to breathe, you know?"

"You can go if you want," Matt says, pulling up the covers and rolling away from me again. "But I'm not going there."

I feel the silly tears come to my eyes. I hate this chasm of theology widening between us. It breaks my heart that where I find solace is where Matt finds reminders of The Assembly. I want to pretend this isn't happening. I want to argue my way out of it, but every time I try to explain myself, it comes out the wrong way.

It has been so long since I've experienced a connection with God. How can I deny the experience I had with Mary in the hospital? How can I deny the relief I felt after praying the Memorare? I want to explore it further, to find out more, but would I have to choose between feeling close to God again and feeling close to my husband?

I go to the bathroom and shower, get dressed, and put on my makeup. Maybe we can't resolve it right now, but I am determined to continue seeking—whatever the cost. A few moments later, Matt taps on the door.

"Let's go to Mass today," he says. "I'm not down with the pope, but I *am* curious."

"Elizabeth, you need to stop talking to your husband about Catholicism," my priest says, chuckling softly behind the confessional screen. "God called *you* to enter the church, and you can let that be enough."

It's been several months since that difficult conversation with Matt, and although he still isn't interested in attending Mass, he's seen how much it means to me. This past Easter, I entered the Catholic Church by myself.

"B-but maybe if I give him the right books, the right arguments, he'll understand that this isn't some infatuation!" I say to the priest through the confessional screen.

"So, how's arguing working for you?" the priest asks.

"Well…"

"Aren't you just confessing all the arguing you've been doing?"

"Um…heh-heh."

"Elizabeth?"

"Yes?"

"No. More. Talking. About. The Church."

"Oh."

"Elizabeth, this is not your job. You don't need to use words. This is the Holy Spirit's job, and you're just getting in the way."

I feel myself blush. "So, just stop?"

"Yes."

"Well…okay…then." I wring my hands and glance at the crucifix. Suddenly, I laugh. A huge wave of relief sweeps over me. Arguing with Matt *isn't* my job. It isn't my responsibility to convince *anyone* of anything. My journey to Catholicism is mine. Am I willing to go on this journey no matter who comes along? If God has drawn me here by His unconditional love, then I can trust God to take care of everything else.

"Your job is to love yourself, love God, and love others," the priest says.

"Thanks, Father."

"For your penance I'd like you to go to the bookstore and buy a book about love. Then meditate on it, okay?"

Read a book? Now, that is my kind of penance.

Chapter 22

I Am Not Afraid

"M"ommy, I'm scared," Jewel says to me as we pull into the church parking lot. I put the minivan in park and stare at the heat waves shimmering up from the asphalt. It's been five years since we left The Assembly. Although I'm now attending Mass, the kids love the youth programs at a nearby Presbyterian church, and this summer, Jewel has pleaded with us to let her attend the summer camp.

"Do you still want to go?" I ask.

She looks at me for a long moment and then says, "Yes."

We unload her sleeping bag and suitcase and make our way toward the registration table. Suddenly, my hands begin to shake and my vision narrows. My stomach clenches into a tight knot. I bow my head and hurry across the lawn, dragging her suitcase behind me. I should have known dropping off my daughter at summer camp would be an anxiety trigger.

I fight the lightning bolt of fear racing through my body. There is a crushing sensation in my chest. *Oh no. Not now!* I don't want Jewel to know I'm having a flashback. *Oh, God, help.* I haul the suitcase under a shady tree and stop abruptly.

"Mommy?"

"Just give me a minute, okay, hon?"

I breathe. I try to force back the images flooding my mind. I use a little mind trick my therapist taught me and imagine a steel door coming down across the stage of my mind. But I can't do it fast enough: *I am five years old at camp, urinating in a muddy trench... I'm so homesick I've lost my appetite. I cry myself to sleep every night and believe I'm going to hell because I love my mother more than I love God.*

"Mommy, we have to check in." My daughter's voice snaps me back to the present, and I force a smile.

We move out of the shade and toward the registration table just as a young girl calls my daughter's name and runs to greet her. I see the anxiety slip away from my daughter's face, and she grins excitedly. The two of them start chattering about being cabin mates. We check in and attach her identification labels to her luggage.

"Bye, Mom!" Jewel says, throwing her arms around my waist. I squeeze her, the tears pricking my eyes. *I don't deserve her love.* I swallow the lump in my throat. "Have a great time," I say. "I'll see you next week!"

Jewel boards the bus with her friends, waving at me. I lean against a nearby tree. I look up. Tiny leaves flutter against a hot summer sky.

The bus roars to life, and I am gripped by a sudden urge to jump onboard, haul Jewel away, rescue her. Keep her safe, safe, safe.

No, she wants to go. She begged to go. "You are not abandoning her," I whisper to myself. "You are safe. She is safe."

I scan the bus windows looking for her face. She is bouncing up and down, talking with her friends. She spots me waving and blows me a kiss. The bus rumbles away and parents cheer.

Their cheering startles me. They're all smiling, convinced their kids will have a wonderful time. They're so trusting.

Some of the parents are chatting about upcoming vacations and what a great day it is for frozen yogurt. They are relaxed and happy.

I can't imagine feeling that way. To me, it seems like I've just survived a life-threatening event. Sending my daughter to camp felt like a herculean task in courage. But nobody seems to notice my trembling hands and teary eyes.

It's okay. I don't want anyone to suspect a thing. All that matters is I fought a huge battle. And I won.

I decide to treat myself to frozen yogurt—just like a normal, healthy person.

I wish I could tell you I'm 100 percent cured. The thing is, becoming healthy requires help and daily work. And time.

I kept thinking I would just "get closure" and move "Onward, Christian Soldiers"! But starting our lives over from scratch, building a life in a new city, raising a large family, and reexamining every belief in order to find a more balanced way of living has been a far greater task than I ever imagined. It wasn't enough to leave The Assembly, or even to find a new church to call home. I had to actively untangle myself from the fundamentalism *inside* me.

And I still do.

Like most children raised in a high-demand environment—whether that's as a result of religion, alcohol, violence, or poverty—I find myself often living on hyperalert, constantly scanning for potential threats. After all, I was raised to see threats everywhere—out there, yes, but also *in here*.

Even today, getting my brain to think new thoughts and beliefs can be an uphill battle. No sooner do I get one part of my brain rewired than some new challenge arises and more "brain surgery" is required.

And then there are the physical side effects. I need daily medication to help me deal with anxiety. And those childhood summers spent at Bible boot camp? Well, let's just say those experiences gave me the gift of lifelong bathroom issues.

I still don't know how to rest or relax. I feel guilty about taking a day off. I fear I'm spiritually lazy if I have margins of downtime. It has taken nearly a decade to realize that living frantically isn't, in fact, a virtue. Or healthy.

To be honest, being a fundamentalist was almost easier because I didn't have to think for myself. Sure, lack of freedom sucked. But at least I could always blame someone higher up when things went wrong. Now, I have to take responsibility for my own life and, um, wow: this whole living-in-freedom-thing is riddled with discomfort! I have to make my own decisions, figure out what I like and dislike, and even (gasp!) make mistakes. I've learned there is no direct, nonstop flight to my own well-being.

I trace my habits of overcommitting and then burning out, of defaulting into black-or-white thinking, and of assuming the worst about everything to the fundamentalist inside me. She is a terrible oppressor. I had to go to Confession eleventy billion times before I finally started receiving forgiveness. And then I had to go to Confession all over again just so I could start forgiving others—mainly my grandfather, my grandma, and my dad.

You see, the fundamentalist inside me doesn't know how to give grace or receive it. But me? I'm learning. Slowly.

I'm so thankful God allows us the freedom to leave places that scare us and find safe places where we can rest.

God is big enough to meet us anywhere.

A few years ago I began blogging about the harmful child-training practices I grew up with. It was important for me to share my firsthand experiences so that the broader community of Christians would become aware of this teaching. To my surprise, speaking out on behalf of children who might still be endangered by these teachings gave me a way to transform my personal pain into service to others. This went a long way in helping me heal from my own sense of loss and regret.

To this day, my main motivation in life is children. I try new things, read new books, and seek new experiences because I want my kids to take full advantage of their second-generation freedom. Sometimes Matt says to me that our commitment to recovery is the kids' best chance at having healthy, successful lives. I think he's right.

Speaking of Matt, he eventually made his way into the Catholic Church—that is, after I shut my pie hole and minded my own beeswax. Finding outer and inner freedom from The Assembly has given us a deeper compassion, respect, and appreciation for each other. Marital therapy and our own individual recovery programs have helped us become more emotionally available to each other. Every day I thank God for this man who has stood faithfully by my side and loved me all the way through.

As for The Assembly, most of the sister churches disbanded in the wake of my family's scandals. There are still a few loosely affiliated Assemblies, but I have no contact with them. Likewise, I've not had any direct contact with my grandparents since that last time I saw them more than ten years ago.

The last I heard, my grandparents had sold their home and moved to a retirement community. They never admitted wrongdoing—despite being confronted by almost all the full-time pastors who served in their ministry.

I know this lack of repentance has been terribly difficult for my dad. There was a moment a few years ago when I saw just how much he'd been hurt too. We were eating Easter dinner when Dad said, in passing, that he knew he could never defy his father or else he'd be disowned. This insight has helped me understand why well-intentioned Assembly leaders and pastors caused pain to others; they were being damaged themselves. Of course, this doesn't excuse their behavior, but at least it helps me understand. It helps me forgive.

My relationship with my parents has been rocky, but we always seem to find a way to work things out. Sometimes we need to give each other space. Sometimes we need to tread delicately. When we're together, we're learning to exercise good personal boundaries. And while healing is an ongoing journey, I'm thankful for the ways my parents have tried to understand my experiences inside The Assembly. They have made changes, and the way they live their lives now gives me hope for our future together.

Each day when I wake up, I lie still for a moment, simply listening to my breath. I thank God for another day, and then I recommit myself to the work of recovery. Well, sometimes I simply commit to taking a nap or giving myself a break. Giving others a break. Smelling the roses. Drinking a glass of fine Pinot Noir.

The only thing I know for sure is that if I want continued healing, I must "act as if" God loves me and has a future for me. It's strange, but it works. The more I choose to believe God loves me, the more loving I believe God is. I am no longer a victim being acted upon. I am now actively participating in loving God, loving myself, and loving others.

I once heard a story about a woman who asked God to move a mountain. God said okay, and then He handed her a shovel. I think that's a good analogy for how my story ends. I'm still shoveling. I'm still uncovering, sorting, reexamining. But I am working on it. And giving it a rest.

I don't believe in perfect closure. But each day, I can choose to take care of myself. I can choose to *let* God love me.

He has given me a future and a hope.

I am not afraid.

I'm winding my way through racks of costumes in my daughter's dressing room. Matt is waiting outside while I make this quick detour to check in with our ballerina. The lighted mirrors reflect a rainbow of tulle and rhinestones.

"Mom! I'm over here!"

I catch my breath. From behind one of the costume racks, Jewel appears, resplendent in a sparkling white tutu. A shining crown glistens on her head. She's been dancing since age three, and tonight, just shy of her thirteenth birthday, she'll perform several pieces on pointe. My mom stands next to Jewel, excitedly snapping pictures.

When she sees me approach, Mom breaks into a huge smile, opens her arms to me. "Oh, Elizabeth. Doesn't Jewel look just lovely?"

I let Mom hug me, taking in her familiar scent. Mom's hair is snowy white now, and wrinkles frame the flash of her bright green eyes. Mom holds me back for a moment and looks me over. "Are you okay, honey?"

"Y-yes," I say, embarrassed by the flood of emotion I'm feeling. Standing here in the bright lights of the dressing room with Jewel's future dazzling our eyes—well, the past seems so far behind us. My mother, me, my daughter: How did we make it this far?

"Isn't she gorgeous?" Mom breathes, her arm wrapped around my waist. We stand together and watch Jewel adjust some pins in her hair.

She spins, light footed, to face us. "I'm so nervous!"

"Oh, honey! You're going to do wonderfully!" Mom says.

"Just remember, American Ballet Theatre accepted you to their summer intensive. You must be fabulous!" I add.

Jewel bursts into laughter. "Okay, you guys. You realize you're both a little biased, right?"

I look at Mom and she laughs. Jewel chuckles and bends to retie the pink ribbons of her pointe shoes. It's almost show time.

Mom turns to me. "Can you believe this?"

I shake my head. I can't believe any of this. Ever since my twins were born, Mom has done nothing but help me. It's as if the attention she was unable to give me as a child she now pours out on my children. Every time she baby-sits, buys my kids outfits, takes them on field trips, or drives Jewel to dance class, a piece of our relationship is restored.

Recently I appeared on Anderson Cooper's daytime TV talk show to discuss the spanking practices taught by Michael Pearl—the same ones we used in The Assembly. After watching the show, Mom asked to speak with me. Her eyes were filled with tears as we sat in my family room. She and Dad had talked, she said. They had examined their actions in The Assembly. They were both sorry for the ways they'd hurt me. Mom handed me a letter. It was from Dad, a letter of apology and contrition. Could I find it in my heart to forgive them?

Could I?

Yes! I needed to forgive. I'd been holding on to my pain for so long that it had somehow become a part of me—I was my pain. I had talked and blogged and written about my pain. It was time for me to let go.

In the dressing room, Mom grabs my hand, pulling me out of my reverie.

"I forgot!" she says. "Dad is waiting outside. Can you go make sure he has his ticket to the show?"

I nod. "Sure."

Jewel looks up at me from her Degas-like pose on the floor. She smiles. "Now, Mom, don't cheer too loud, okay?"

"Baby, I'm gonna blow the roof off."

"Mom!"

"Okay. I won't cheer. Too loudly."

As it turns out, I can't even cheer at all. When the curtain rises and my ballerina dances on pointe, all I can do is behold her shimmering beauty. All I can see is the woman she is becoming, graceful and free. All I can do is marvel at the mother who gave me life, the Mother who brought me back to God, and this beautiful ballerina who made me a mother.

In the dark of the theater, Matt reaches for my hand, and together we watch our daughter dance.

Here we all are.

The future is open wide.

Author's Note

By the time I was a teenager in 1992, The Assembly was profiled in a book called *Churches That Abuse*. The abuses grew worse and went unchecked. In 2003, most Assembly churches disbanded after my uncle's violence came to light along with the stories of my grandfather's adulteries.

Of course, a quick summary of The Assembly's thirty-three-year history can't convey the deep, personal impact it had on thousands of lives—especially those of children who were born and raised inside it. *Girl at the End of the World* is my attempt to tell that smaller story, the story of a child coming to awareness inside a closed system and her struggle for physical, spiritual, and emotional freedom.

All the things I write about really happened, and yet my story is not an unbiased account. It is simply *my* experience. To that end, scenes and dialogue have been reconstructed. Especially in part 1, events follow a thematic arc rather than strict chronological order.

I've checked my memories against the twenty-plus diaries I kept while growing up and continued a decade-long conversation with some of my closest friends and family members who also grew up in The Assembly. To protect privacy, I have changed the names and identifying details of most people who appear in these pages.

My goal in writing this book is to shed light on the subtle forms of spiritual and religious abuse. I can only hope that my story brings a measure of solace, hope, and solidarity to anyone who has experienced a similarly painful church experience. May it sing freedom to captives and healing for those who have been bruised in the name of God.

Discussion Questions

1. Elizabeth defines a cult as something that "destroys the God-given freedom of each person...usually through fear." Have you ever been involved in a cult-like group, whether it was religious or not? How did its leader(s) attempt to control its followers? If, like Elizabeth, you'd been taught strict obedience to a human leader, how would you have responded? What do you think of her statement at age nine: "I am ready to die for Jesus"?

2. Papa George "claimed his authority came straight from God—which was just another way of saying he ordained himself... Papa George was pretty much a prophet, priest, and king all rolled into one." Can a person ordain himself? What are the dangers involved in a self-proclaimed prophet or leader? How did George exercise a king's authority? What was the result?

3. After revealing the family meeting spot for use if the Antichrist arrested Elizabeth's parents, her father drives Elizabeth home, and she "silently ask[s] Jesus into my heart—for the 8,364th time." Have you known anyone with a religious experience as full of fear as Elizabeth's was? What role do you think fear plays in religion? Is it useful? necessary? destructive?

4. What do you think of the rules enforced on Sister Kathleen in the Geftakys' training home, such as no pierced ears, no immodest clothing, daily Scripture reading, punishment for serving dinner ten min-

utes late, and answering to the Head Steward? Do such rules help a person attain godliness? If so, how? What rules did you grow up with—and how did they affect you?

5. At one point Elizabeth concludes, "God doesn't want me to be happy. He wants me to be holy." Is this true? Are the two states really mutually exclusive, or can a person be both happy and holy? Describe someone who embodies only one of these qualities and someone who has both. Which one are you?

6. How did you respond to the Assembly dictum of daily spankings, starting when children are six months old? Do you think "breaking the will" is essential to a child's well-being? Do you believe children are "inherently wicked sinners"? What do you think about the "obedience tests" Grandma Betty encouraged mothers to set up? How were you trained—and was it effective?

7. In chapter 7, Elizabeth learns that "being a pacifist means hitting your kid to save her soul from hell but *not* hitting an intruder to save her life." If a person uses violence as a tool but vocally abhors it at the same time, what message does that send? What is the result? Has a double standard ever been imposed on your life? How did it impact you?

8. How did you feel when you read about Elizabeth waking to an empty house and her panic that the Rapture had occurred? Have you ever faced the same fear? What is a healthy, balanced attitude toward the End Times?

9. When Elizabeth lies about her relationship with Aristotle, her father declares, "Your behavior is jeopardizing everything God has for you.

Do you really want to miss out on God's eternal plan for your life?" Do you agree—do you think "God's eternal plan" can be easily way-laid? If so, what are some means of missing God's will? Has anyone ever accused you of doing that?

10. After they're married, Elizabeth and her husband face colliding goals, pressure to follow harsh parenting guidelines, and occasional appearances of "Assembly Matt." Why do you think Matt acted the way he did? How was he like Elizabeth yet different from her? Did you feel hopeful or afraid for the couple as time went on?

11. Were you surprised when Elizabeth embraced Mary as a source of help and hope? What do you think of her conclusion, "Jesus has sent His Mother to comfort me"? If you are Protestant, have you ever thought of Mary as a heroic beacon of the faith, or like Elizabeth, have you celebrated only the leading male figures of the Bible? Why?

12. "The gentler I was with myself, the safer I felt." Elizabeth learns through therapy how to ease the self-loathing she's been taught in The Assembly. When do you feel safe? What kinds of people, actions, or thoughts bring you security? What does safety look like for you?

A Conversation with the Author

Elizabeth, I was deeply moved when reading your story. Even though I wasn't raised in a cult, I can relate a lot to this book because of similar brokenness I've experienced in my life and the lives of people I love dearly. I laughed, I wept, and I was healed through reading such a raw, real description of living in a spiritually abusive, manipulative environment. So as we start off our interview, I just wanted to ask, What was it like writing this book? How hard was it to rehash your life story, to be so brutally honest about yourself and your family's life inside The Assembly?

Next to birthing my five children, this book was by far the hardest thing I've ever done. For one thing, I really underestimated the toll it would take on me. It was extremely difficult and emotionally exhausting to relive these experiences. Especially when I was writing about some of the early childhood experiences. Sometimes at the end of writing these scenes I had to physically "shake off" my little girl or fourteen-year-old teenager or young housewife and do something to bring me back into my current, happy life. I usually took a long, hot bath because writing about these painful things made me very cold. I also read lots of fiction novels to help take my brain *out* of my past.

Eventually, though, the pain was just so real every single day that it kinda brought my body down to a depressed state. When I was in The Assembly, I was depressed and anxious all the time. Writing the book brought me back to that dark place, and it was really difficult to pull myself out of it.

I am so thankful for my husband who—on the worst days—sat with me as I took my hot bath, brought me food, let me take naps, and encouraged me to do whatever I needed to do to finish this project. I am also thankful for my exercise friends who encouraged me to keep working out through the whole book-writing process. Running and hard exercise really kept me sane. And so did my therapist, my psychiatrist, and my antidepressant medication! Pretty much, I couldn't have done this alone.

A lot of people are confused as to how fundamentalism fits into the bigger picture of Christianity. Do you have any insight into the core characteristics of fundamentalism and how to help people understand what you're talking about when you critique Christian fundamentalism in your book?

What I'm critiquing is not so much adherence to orthodox belief, but the *way* in which these beliefs are practiced and the systems that are created for enforcing/punishing those who "break the rules." The fundamentalist mind-set is, quite simply, a graceless mind-set. It doesn't give second chances. It is black and white. It operates on the assumption that everyone deserves hell and everyone is inherently evil. In my experience, fundamentalism flourishes when one personality is given God-like status and everyone believes this pastor speaks for God. The thing is, fundamentalism can happen anywhere—not just in strict churches but in megachurches too. It's more about a mind-set and a way of operating than it is about the particular beliefs.

So fundamentalism is not simply a religious problem. Can you give some signs of fundamentalism in the context of a larger world? What does that look like? What signs should people be aware of?

Well, my husband and I sometimes joke that organized sports are fundamentalist cults! We've encountered teams where a charismatic

leader/coach rules with an iron fist. There are codes of silence and intimi-
dation, and apparently winning a game excuses all kinds of harmful treatment: yelling, threatening, and blaming. I think fundamentalism is a
human problem—a human tendency—and we must watch for it no matter which social group we interact with. Warning signs: a leader/coach/
CEO whose behavior goes unchecked, where there is no balance of power
or outside accountability, where rules are arbitrary and enforced unfairly,
an environment where questions are discouraged and loyalty is the pre-
eminent virtue.

**You see this playing out in politics all the time too. America is very
prone to fundamentalism. It's such a human problem to want to
go to extremes and make everyone else the enemy. So what is a
balance between healthy questioning and rebellion?**

Yes, I agree about politics. It's very much a sickness in our society. I
think a fundamentalist mind-set only leads to deeper polarization. We've
lost the ability to listen to the other side, to help us understand and learn
from each other. A true leader will be humble so that if you're asking
questions, you're not going to feel like you're committing a sin in doing
so. You shouldn't have to choose between asking questions and being
considered rebellious. That leads to an environment of fear and silence. A
safe environment always welcomes questions. A safe leader is not intimi-
dated by questions.

**Speaking of safe environments, I found it so interesting how you
point out the women in The Assembly changed the way they communicated the longer they were in it. They couldn't voice real
opinions or thoughts or "speak like men." How long did it take you
to learn to find your voice after you left? When did you start your
blog?**

I started my blog in November 2006, and it took me several years of experimentation to start feeling comfortable with voicing my opinions and ideas. At first, I was going to be the typical mommy blogger—crafts and parenting tips and stuff. I had no intention of ever writing anything about my upbringing. So many of the blogs I was reading were Christian moms, a lot of homeschooling Christians, etc., and I started seeing that the mind-set of The Assembly was everywhere. It was found in so many Christian circles. These alarm bells started going off in my head. I started commenting on these blogs and saying, "I'm not really sure that's right." The push-back from my comments made me start thinking, *Why am I feeling upset about these issues?* It forced me to start thinking about my upbringing and what was wrong with it.

I also started using my full name, Elizabeth, instead of little-girl nicknames like Liz or Lizzie. I intentionally blogged under my first and middle name, Elizabeth Esther, to take ownership of my name. It was superimportant for me to be *my own person,* and my husband was secure enough not to mind that I still don't use my married name as my writing name. I also had to get over my fear of making mistakes. I now give myself permission to make mistakes, learn from them, and grow. But learning to own my name and voice is an ongoing process. I still struggle with the belief that I shouldn't be speaking. I experience self-doubt almost daily. I still can't believe I somehow got a book deal!

Obviously, you've raised some controversy over things you have said on your blog. The more you've raised your voice, the more push-back you've gotten. How have you handled all the criticism?

Oddly enough, my upbringing in The Assembly helped me in that regard. I was raised preaching on a street corner with people yelling at me all the time. I just had to learn that not everyone is going to agree with me.

There are people who will hate you. You've got to know who you are and be okay saying it. I learned that at an early age.

The tone on my blog has changed quite a bit over the years because I've healed a lot. I don't feel like I have to be on the defensive. So I'm learning that I'm willing to listen to what critics say because I usually can learn something from it. I've learned to own what parts of my words I need to change and what I need to stay true to.

Talk to me more about purity culture. It's a hot topic in the church right now and one you've had lots of thoughts on. The scene in your book at youth group where the leaders give you the modesty talk was pretty hilarious—not going to lie. It reminds me of several modesty talks I received while growing up. How have you processed and healed from purity culture? What do you hope to teach your girls and boys about the concept of sexuality?

I appreciate the Catholic view of sexuality because it doesn't compartmentalize the person. Our sexuality is about our *whole* person—not exclusively focused on the way we dress. I think the main problem with purity culture was its exclusivity of focus and emphasis. By focusing so myopically on modest dress and codes of conduct, it was easy to forget that sexuality is about relationship. It's about our relationships to ourselves, to God, and to others. Sexuality, like *all* parts of our humanity, is about living in wholeness and consistency. I am grateful I was a virgin when I was married. Being a virgin saved me some heartache. I am grateful I learned self-control. I still believe saving sexual behavior for marriage is good and right and best honors ourselves, God, and others.

So then what does a whole-person view of sexuality mean? What does it mean to not be focused on the outward appearances, the modesty rules, etc.?

Modesty encompasses all of how we live—how we steward our finances, how we eat, how we treat others, how we respect our privacy and the privacy of others. It's a whole-person approach to the virtue of modesty. It's not just female focused. It's not about how much women should be covering up. It's about how humans should be spending their time and resources, how they exude a sense of humility and wisdom in all their actions.

The Bible was used as a weapon to manipulate and control you for so long. I think it's a foreign concept to many that some people might need to distance themselves from Scripture for a while in order to heal. Do you think this might be why you were so drawn to Catholicism—since it's not based on *sola scriptura* but also on church and tradition? What are the best ways you spiritually connect now with God? Do you find you can put the Bible back into your life?

Actually, what most surprised me about Catholicism was how much Scripture was read during the Mass. There are actually more Scripture readings during Mass than there were in many of the Protestant churches I visited and attended. But Catholics handle the Bible much differently—dare I say, more reverently? Scripture is read with reverence and without a bunch of personal interpretation added onto it. The cantor sings the psalm. We stand for the Gospel reading. For the first time in my life, I was able to *hear* the Scripture because it wasn't being filtered through the interpretation of a human. It was just being read aloud. This healed me so much. In fact, it healed me so much that I now serve as a lector at my parish—meaning I read the Scripture during Mass. I so enjoy reading Scripture now because each day there is a prescribed reading and it allows me to sink into the Word without feeling like I need to explain it, dissect it, or filter it. I can just drink the Word.

I find it interesting that one prominent evangelical recently said that Protestants actually have more spiritual abuse in their churches than Catholics, even though Catholics usually get the bad reputation. In some ways, this makes sense because many Protestants have little leadership structure other than their own pastors, while Catholicism has a built-in leadership structure. Do you see the Catholic Church as less abusive than Protestantism? Why would that be? Do you feel safer now that you're a Catholic? If so, why?

I'm glad I wasn't the one who said that, because I attract enough controversy as it is! But yes, what a great insight, and I absolutely agree. In fact, this was a *huge* reason why I joined the Catholic Church. I felt absolutely safe there. Regardless of what the media says, the Catholic Church has taken great care in making reparation for the sexual abuse scandals. In my parish, for example, even volunteers like me have to be background checked *and* fingerprinted. And as far as spiritual abuse goes, there isn't room for individual personalities to attract big followings because of our built-in authority structure. It just doesn't happen. There's a reason why you don't hear about Father So-and-So who built a *huge* mega-Catholic-parish all by himself! This is not to say there aren't politics and popular priests, but things don't devolve so terribly as they do in pastor-centric churches where the sole arbiter between God and man is Mr. Popular Pastor.

You're right that often the sole arbiter between God and man is Mr. Popular Pastor! Cults and unhealthy churches manifest this idea that *the church you're involved in* equals *God in your life.* Or *the pastor's voice* equals *God's voice to you.* Give me your thoughts on this. How have you learned to differentiate between God and a church or pastor because of your childhood experiences?

It took me a long time to arrive at this superprofound conclusion, but one day I *finally* realized that nobody is God but God! Imagine that. So, whenever I hear *anyone*—pastor or otherwise—starting to talk as if he or she is God's special mouthpiece, I just take it with about ten gallons of salt. I used to feel threatened by other pastors' understandings of God, but that doesn't worry me anymore. The more I invest in my own relationship with God, the less bothered I am by what other people say He is or isn't like. It's like that verse from St. John 10:27: "My sheep hear my voice." I know the voice of my Shepherd now. I know how to recognize it, and I can tell the difference between my Shepherd speaking and someone trying to speak for Him.

Okay, so let's talk about love. I was really touched by the story of you and Matt. Even in the most abusive and manipulative of situations, you two somehow found a sincere, blossoming relationship. You've said before on your blog that it's a miracle you and your husband are still together because of the environment you came from. Can you elaborate on this? What things have you and Matt done to help heal together as a couple?

Matt and I have been through hell and high water. Also a lot of therapy. We've done marital therapy, individual therapy, and we each attend our own twelve-step groups. I really have no explanation for how or why we remained together other than the miraculous, unmerited grace of God. We've both made tons of mistakes—well, I've made more than he has!—but all I can say is that Matt is an especially tenacious lover, a steadfast and noble spirit who has always, always believed the best and seen the best in me and in our future together. We've had our share of heartbreaks and fights and tears, but in the end I just admire my man. I can't help it! I admire him! On a side note about Matt: I've been criticized for not writing about him enough on my blog. People want to know: "If you love him so much, why don't you write about him?" Well, there is a reason for this! Matt is a *very* private introvert. And what we share is so sacred to me that I just keep him to myself. He is my own precious treasure, and frankly, no words can do him justice. So there. That's why I only write about him in my book!

That's beautiful. So maybe one of the reasons you've survived as a couple is because you were both willing to take the steps necessary to heal. Matt had to make the decision to engage and process the situation as much as you did. I also thought it interesting that the priest asked you to be patient with Matt and not push the Catholic Church on him. How hard was that for you? Was it another step in learning to heal, in learning to not push your own spirituality on someone else?

It was *extremely* difficult. One of the hardest things I've ever done. Imagine finding this place where you are so happy, you feel so loved and safe, and you want to share it with the most important person in your life…and he just doesn't want it at all. I had to really learn about respecting boundaries. I had to step back and treat him with all the feelings and actions of love even if he never converted to Catholicism. I had to say, "Even if he never goes to Mass, I must treat him with dignity and honor." Everyone needs to have their own free will and make their own choices about God and their lives. Far be it from me to repeat the mistakes of my childhood by forcing my spiritual decisions on someone else!

It really was an example of how life is very messy. Even when I was writing the book, I really thought Matt would never enter the church. I had to really let go of it. Finally, I just decided that if God wanted it, it would happen. And eventually, it happened.

One of the most powerful scenes in the book is when you are in the bathroom with your daughter and you choose not to spank her and repeat the cycle of abuse. This reminds me so much of the story of Joseph in Genesis. His family had generations of unhealthy relationships, but he chose to put an end to it. Beautiful! What would you like to say to anyone who is facing generational family abuse?

I would say this: just take one step at a time. That moment in the bathroom with my daughter *was* a turning point for me. But it was just the beginning. Breaking the cycle of abuse didn't happen in just one moment. It took several years of repeated steps *away* from that environment before I was fully free. Sometimes I felt bad about how slowly it took to change this. I wanted things to change quickly! I wanted *freedom now*! But God wasn't moving on my time schedule. I had a lot of waiting to do. A lot of trusting. One step at a time. One day at a time. One hour at a time. Some changes happen overnight, yes, but most lasting changes take many years. It's okay to take the long route.

I've often described healing and breaking abusive patterns as walking around a mountain. You keep walking in circles and seem to be at the same places you were before, but you're always a little higher up. Have you found this to be true?

Yes, I see what you're saying! For example, with my daughter, I'd been pressured into disciplining her by spanking. I did continue to spank for a while. But later on, I asked myself, "Do I need to spank this much? No, I don't, because it's not effective." Then later it was, "Now I'm going to spank only for these certain infractions." Then it was, "What are other alternatives?" Eventually, it got to the point where I was spanking only once or twice a year.

Also, for Matt and me—we were such a mess when we first got out of The Assembly. We had to really learn to give each other space and gradually grow together.

I like to say, "Progress, not perfection." If you're making progress, you're still not being perfect, but you're moving forward.

Your connection with Mother Mary was profound and refreshing to me, as I'm not Catholic and have never had much of an interaction with the concept of Mary. How has Mary continued to help you heal?

Oh, Mary! I love her! Oh, how I love her! Yes, Mary has continued to heal and soothe and calm all my fears. She is the always merciful Mother to whom I can run and pour out all my fears and worries, knowing she will listen, knowing she prays for me. She never judges; she never condemns. But one prick from her sorrowful eyes is enough to convict my heart and help me continue to trust her Son, my Savior. This relationship to Mary was completely cut off to me while I was in a male-dominated Christian environment. Protestantism, as a whole, is sort of male dominated with the great beacons of faith being Martin Luther, John Calvin, Dwight Moody, John Piper, etc. It's all men all the time! For one thing, it was almost impossible for me to hear Scripture without male voices booming in my ears.

I agree! Many women have a deep ache to feel understood in the church, but when it is so male dominated, they often feel alone. It's so important to have women's voices. So have there been other female figures in the church you've looked to for healing?

I have grown deeply fond of women like St. Thérèse of Lisieux, whose unapologetic emotional outbursts of love for God are revered among Catholics. She wrote an autobiography called *The Story of a Soul*. She was very emotional; she felt things very deeply. What she was known for is a concept called "The Little Way." Any small act of kindness, a smile, etc., was to show God's love. I connected with that because I am so emotional, and to realize that there is a space in the faith community for emotion allows me to be myself. People aren't telling me that I'm irrational or need to change my femininity. There's this welcoming of femininity, a welcoming of who women are, and that means a lot to me. Also, look at St. Teresa of Avila...St. Joan of Arc! All these women were *allowed* to be their full female selves—emotions and visions and prophecies and all! I so cherish this!

Toward the end of the book, you choose to let God love you. Your story reminds me of 1 John 4:18: "There is no fear in love; but perfect love casts out fear, because fear involves punishment, and the one who fears is not perfected in love" (NASB). I think this is a huge problem in the church today. We tend to relate to God through fear and punishment. I'd love to hear more of your thoughts on this and your experiences with learning to walk in God's love. What does accepting God's love really mean?

The first step is to see yourself as God sees you. When God looks at me, He looks at me with the eye of love. I am delightful to Him! He is delighted in me! He *loves* to see me live my life! And as I begin to understand how God sees me, I am able to love and accept myself. God doesn't want me hating myself or disliking myself, because He sees me as a beautiful child—His own precious creation. Then, as I love myself I am able to love others. Letting God love us is the key to everything. Once we can receive His love, we are filled up to overflowing and eagerly share that unconditional love with everyone we meet.

You stood up to your grandfather and grandmother about the abuse before you left The Assembly. You also confronted Michael

Pearl about his discipline methodology on TV on Anderson Cooper's talk show. I couldn't imagine what that would've been like—to face the people who had been the cause of so much of your abuse growing up. Which was harder to face? What did you learn by confronting them?

Hmm. I haven't thought about which one was harder; that's a good question. Both situations were difficult in different ways.

With Michael Pearl, it was happening in this false environment on a TV stage. I knew I had to parse my words down to some nice-sounding sound bite. We couldn't get deep down into the true issues. But if he had listened to the constant stream of people's complaints over the years, we wouldn't have been in that situation. So I just had to put on my bullet-proof vest, so to speak, and speak out for the children. Michael was more impersonal to me. He represents the figurehead of the discipline movement. Yet he wasn't my family. So in that regard, I was able to depersonalize the situational and think, *I'm just going in for the children.*

In my grandparents' case, I was going into my family. It was personal. I knew they weren't going to give an inch. We had to go into it with a stack of proof because they weren't going to listen.

But one thing was very similar: both Michael Pearl and my grandparents were extremely prideful. They not only believed they were 100 percent right, they refused to even acknowledge they had perhaps made *any* mistakes and hurt people. All of us make mistakes. But the harm is only multiplied when we adamantly resist hearing the entreaties of those we've wounded. Both of these situations were tragic because they were so unnecessary. If enough people in your flock are pointing out concerns to you, you really need to check yourself and ask, "What are my blind spots? Where do I need to grow? What might I be doing wrong?"

I continue to pray for the Pearls' repentance and my grandparents' repentance. It's not too late!

You're no longer the "girl at the end of world"! So what's next for you? What would you like to see happen in the coming years as you continue to step forward into a future with hope? What's in store for you and your family?

Oh my. Well, my three older children will be entering the Catholic Church this Easter, Lord willing. I'm so excited about that! I love teaching and speaking, so I'm hoping to share my story with others and encourage them to not give up hope in seeking a loving God. My oldest daughter has dreams of being accepted to a ballet company, and I love supporting her in that. And when I'm not running around with the kids, teaching, writing, or speaking, I help my husband run his second job: a commercial cleaning company. Our lives are full and I wouldn't have it any other way—except, of course, I want to write more books, host my own talk show or TV show, adopt more rescue dogs, plant a garden, keep chickens, have a pygmy goat, and adopt children! I love *everything*!

That sounds amazing. Do it all! So I'm curious... What do you want to write about next?

Well, this burning thing in my heart right now has a lot to do with emotional and spiritual healing. I'm hoping to write about that and what it means. *How to find your center of stillness and peace. How to listen to your feelings.* God gave you these things for a reason.

I also want to write more about Mary and other women in the church. There are so many female saints whom I didn't know about for years. I didn't realize there are thousands of years of female voices in the church. I feel as if God is leading me to talk about them. I think what God's doing now in the church is bringing to the front the voices of women. The next revival in the church will be through women. We don't want the division anymore that men have been bringing to the church for so long. I'm really interested in seeing the relational love and unity that Jesus speaks about come through in women.

Well, whatever it ends up being, I can't wait to read your next book! Thanks so much for being one of those women who has been brave enough to raise her voice and incite change in the church.

For more information about Elizabeth Esther please visit www.ElizabethEsther.com.

Interview by **Teryn O'Brien.** Teryn works in marketing with various imprints of Penguin Random House LLC and occasionally writes articles for several online magazines. She spends her free time roaming the mountains of Colorado, writing a series of novels, and combating sex trafficking. Read her blog on embracing one's identity, healing from pain, and the joys of creativity at www.terynobrien.com. You can also follow her on Twitter @TerynOBrien or connect with her on Facebook (TerynOBrienWriter).

Acknowledgments

When I was a child dreaming of becoming a writer, I imagined myself writing Nancy Drew mysteries or novels like *Anne of Green Gables*. Writing a highly personal memoir about my life inside fundamentalism was *not* the plan. Still, for my love of reading and writing, I owe a debt of gratitude to my mother. She drove me to the library each week and said yes whenever I asked her to buy me more books. Thank you, Mom. I love you.

Dad, I admire your idealistic, adventurous spirit and thank you for bringing that sense of exploration and excitement to my life. You taught me to take risks. I love you.

My sister, D: Thank you for understanding why I needed to write this, and thank you for always keeping your tender, loyal, merciful heart. When I grow up, I want to be like you.

My cousins, R, D, and R: We did it. We survived! Here's to a life of thriving in freedom.

Matt: My husband, my anchor, my most faithful one. Thank you for your unfailing patience, steadiness, and relentless optimism. I love you, always.

Jewel, James, Jude, Jorai, and Jasiel: Thank you for giving me the privilege and honor of being your mama. You five are my truest treasures. Also, thank you for bringing me water with lemons in it and asking, "Are you done with your book *yet*?"

My agent, Rachelle Gardner: You found me, believed in me, and encouraged me when I felt like giving up. Thank you.

My editors, David and Heather Kopp: You knew exactly how to pace me, when to push me, and when to let go. You taught me I am loved and I am safe. Thank you for bearing with my prickly, intense personality. Also for patiently listening to my multiple weepy freak-outs—ahem. I love you both so very, very much.

My blog readers: You were my first real audience. I stumbled and fumbled and somehow found my voice through your generous grace. You are my people. Thank you for coming back again and again even when I made mistakes, lost my temper in the comment box, or totally screwed things up. I love you!

Several teachers encouraged me in my craft, and I would like to thank them here: Mr. Wiegman, my kind, wonderful high school English teacher; and my favorite college English professors at Cal State Fullerton: Dr. Susan Jacobsen, Dr. John Brugaletta, Dr. Cornel Bonca, and, in loving memory, Dr. Atara Stein.

Last, without the love and support of the following writers and friends, this book would not have happened: Matthew Paul Turner, Rachel Held Evans, Jennifer Fulwiler, Sarah Bessey, Nish Weiseth, Ann Voskamp, Sarah Mae, Josh Riebock, Adam McHugh, Kristen Howerton, Stephanie and David Drury, Enoch and Raulna Y., Margaret Irons, Brent and Suzie Trockman, Diane Stratman, Hillary McFarland, Katherine Ray, Eden F., Hannah C., Joel and Jennifer Feeser, Margaret M., Stacey Weld, Elise B., Brian T., Sandra Miranda and all the wonderful people at Hit the Mark Fitness Bootcamp. Many, many thanks to my dear therapist, MR, for keeping me safe; my psychiatrist, AM, for keeping me sane; and all my companions in recovery for keeping me honest.

All my love,
EE